"*The Fear* is a hybrid memoir and cultural study, which uses the personal to reach into the depths of the psychology of fear. Artist and writer Christiana Spens explores how fear impacts our lives — from the personal to the political, through gender politics to terrorism — referring to images, art, films, philosophy and more. The memoir aspect is written with intellectual detachment creating almost a fable of fear, that space 'between fear and anxiety' — at once a psychological study and an intimate portrayal of a woman making sense of the world. It is a finely tuned, fascinating interrogation of an emotion that hijacks us all. Both intimate and psychologically rigorous, *The Fear* pushes the bounds of memoir into intellectual territory."

— **Lily Dunn**, author of *Sins of My Father*

THE FEAR

THE FEAR

Christiana Spens

Published by Repeater Books

An imprint of Watkins Media Ltd

Unit 11 Shepperton House

89-93 Shepperton Road

London

N1 3DF

United Kingdom

www.repeaterbooks.com

A Repeater Books paperback original 2023

1

Distributed in the United States by Random House, Inc., New York.

Copyright © Christiana Spens 2023

Christiana Spens asserts the moral right to be identified as the author of this work.

Author photo credit: Sophie Davidson

Illustrations by the author

ISBN: 9781914420450

Ebook ISBN: 9781914420535

Printed and bound in the United Kingdom by TJ Books Limited

For my son and my friends.

In memory of my father.

"Though I walk through the valley of the shadow of death,
I will fear no evil, for thou art with me."
— Psalm 23:4

"For beauty is nothing but
the beginning of terror, that we are still able to bear,
and we reserve it so, because it calmly disdains
to destroy us."
— Rainer Maria Rilke

"If you stare too long into the abyss, the abyss stares back."
— Fredrich Nietzsche

Contents

Preface

In Fuseli's painting *The Nightmare* (1790-1), a woman lies rapturously and receptively on a bed, as an incubus sits on her chest and a horse emerges from her bedroom curtains. Revealing an interior world of erotic obsession and infatuation, albeit ambiguous and subconscious, this is a Romantic exploration of desire and dreams.[1] The woman is in a sort of sleep, or delirium, captivated by a haunting, impish and yet domineering demon.

This disturbing dream, as Fuseli depicts it, reveals the war between Enlightenment and Romantic values in the human psyche, and the fact that we cannot rid ourselves of either force. There is no Enlightenment without the deep, instinctual reckoning of chaos, no perfection in beauty without the will to order life, if not necessarily the ability (or intention) to fully compose it. The desire to transform, morph, emerge — to affect awe-inspiring, terrifying change drives us across our movements and philosophies, and drips into these subjects, sustaining their cataclysmic personal revolutions; Fuseli captures the horror of personal transformation and the splintering of the self, the dance between reason and madness, awareness and repression. In this way, *The Nightmare* speaks to

---

1   Christopher Frayling, "Fuseli's The Nightmare: Somewhere between the Sublime and the Ridiculous," in *Gothic Nightmares: Fuseli, Blake, and the Romantic Imagination*, London: Tate Publishing, 2006, 9.

Jungian thought, and the idea of a shadow side — a part of oneself that is not seen clearly, even by ourselves, and which we therefore find projected onto others and the world around us. It is a weighty, haunting, compelling thing, like the sitting incubus, rendering us passive and tormented, confused, as we flail around, half-heartedly seeking to contain it. Fuseli's vision here, his nightmare, encompasses much of what I describe in this book as 'the Fear' — a shadow side of the self that is often repressed, and yet unignorably present. It is a living nightmare, at times — a sense of being trapped, and yet compelled, stifled and fascinated by the depths of its darkness.

The Fear, as I will go on to describe, is also in some ways similar to the state recorded in Sartre's *Nausea*: an encroaching, inescapable feeling that reality itself (when so much of this nightmare is projected onto the outside world) is impossible and incompatible with the self, leading to chronic alienation and isolation. Thoughts and feelings are entangled in this state; thoughts emerge as a rush, a panic, a loop. Logic fails to help, really, to ground or contain these problems in any significant, lasting way; reason itself becomes an intrusive thought amongst many. Reason itself, or a need to be reasonable, is not actually the problem, or at least it alone cannot solve it. I think therefore I do not want to be, I feel therefore I do not want to be — at least not in this moment, not here. Only distortion and denigration will make it bearable. A sense of paralysis and despair leads to humility, though, we find, and the death of the ego, towards true development of oneself. Not only goodness can save us, but the experience and reconciliation of both dark and light, both the shadow and one's brighter, more visible self.

What is the Fear, then? It is this shadow, this emotional state — sometimes felt as an affliction, battled as a demon.

What is this book? It is a record of living through these states and trying to escape them — a philosophical journey, a meditation, a desperate, and often futile attempt to be free. It was fuelled by a desire for this state to end, and a need to know why it persisted, why in spite of myself and my efforts, I spent so many years repeating myself, probing further into the darkness, apparently unable, or on some level unwilling, to let go of a fascination with this state and an equation with clinging, possessive, demonic behaviour with an ultimate freedom from it. A desire to compartmentalise it? To catch it, to celebrate it, even? To reconcile with this shadow side, as it were. To recognise and probe the death wish, that desire to discard, to find freedom in picking it apart. To find out why we − I − am compelled to live this way, to be trapped by myself, by my memories, by my relationships with others. Can I write myself out of it? Can I write the demons down? Can I bring myself to ask them to leave, to crush them, to believe in a brighter life? Can I recover?

I cannot write frankly about many of those experiences and people who have caused me the most fear and pain, ironically, and who helped create, in my own life, for many years, the spectre I write about here. For while each of us has our own personal shadow, our own darkness we must take accountability for, we also have people who inflict theirs upon us, without our consent or want, often quite unthinkingly. The shadow, or the Fear, while it is within, is also deepened and defined by actual people and memories, real threats, whether immediate or remembered.

In this book, I can only skirt the edges of that aspect of the Fear, really. I can mention some experiences but not others, I cannot say everything there is to say. I can just say what it feels like to be terrorised, and what it feels like to see it in others. I can tell you what it does to people, how it defines social behaviour and politics, how it manifests on these many levels in human societies as well as individual psyches. I can write about the reality of living with injustice, in a world in which people are very rarely made accountable or take accountability for their actions, to the point where the world can seem effectively lawless.

I can write about other people in my life a little. But mostly, I have chosen to write about my own feelings, and how relationships with other people, especially those shadowed with bereavement or abuse, are entangled with the individual, the political and the cultural. I hope I can show what the Fear is and what it does, how we cannot understand fear without seeing it as entwined with disassociation, the persistent denial of reality (whether through ourselves or others), and how unequal power dynamics both enable this and flourish under it. Most crucially, perhaps, researching and writing *The Fear* taught me about how power is won and maintained, and the role of our emotional lives in wider political realities.

The Fear is a state of being blinkered and stunted, too paralysed to function, let alone thrive. Although to have a shadow side, one's own darkness, can be an individual concern, it is also how we are kept down by others, because it is where we are vulnerable. In social and political terms, it is how exploitation succeeds. It is the ultimate weapon and injury of psychological warfare. The Fear can be vampiric and sapping, a losing of oneself and others; it can be impossible to fully inhabit oneself, and in this state, to find and enjoy true camaraderie and love. To live with such threat and paralysis is to experience a slow stealing of one's imagination, of the hope that the world can be better, and this is often achieved through nefarious, complex means.

The Fear is the emotional reality of oppression, whether it manifests as an individual battle with repressed memories and desires, or overt socio-political conflicts. It can take on many forms, but in my own life and studies, articulating it in this way, as the Fear — leaning into a Romantic and Jungian understanding of this shadow side — has enabled me to better understand the nature of oppression as well as the subconscious, and therefore, a way out of it.

The Fear is the beginning of resistance. It is a voice within saying "no", demanding a different reality to this one. It is a desire to escape but with nowhere to go; it is the insistence, regardless, that there must be somewhere, even if it is imaginary, at first. In writing this book, my aim was to start drawing a map out of this state, which I know is shared by so many, and to find a real escape route, a path to follow, a means of drawing and writing oneself out of an impossible time.

Heartbreakers

After I graduated, I worked as an au pair in Paris. I was looking after an eighteen-month-old and a six-year-old in the 20th arrondissement. I lived a forty-minute bus ride away, in Montmartre, subletting my room from a French banker, Gilles, and his Russian girlfriend, Tatiana. She seemed to be in a perpetual internship at his bank, and I was told that she needed to improve her English, as part of the wider project to improve her life, directed by him. My fluency in English was the main reason I was chosen to rent out their spare room; for merely chatting in my mother tongue, I would have a reduced rent. My room was tiny, but it overlooked the Sacré-Coeur, and there were rumours Picasso had lived on the same street once.

The children I were looking after also needed to improve their English (and that was also why I was in a job), but they were less enthusiastic about it. I pushed the pram around, anyway, learning "baby French" and trying to stop the older sister from destroying everything while I attended to her younger sister. She definitely did not want to learn English, and in the end, only the baby picked anything up — albeit limited to "nose" and "please", which was somehow enough to impress their mother.

Outside of my new childcare duties, I met some friends — other expats, mostly — writing their novels and making their films or planning them, usually teaching or babysitting as well. I collected numbers of waiters and let my flatmates match-make me with their strange friends out of politeness, but to no avail. I was infatuated with an unavailable man, but I hadn't told them that. He was too old for me and had a girlfriend. Gradually, over the months of unrequited, misplaced infatuation, I broke down in pastels and puddles, becoming one more cliché in a city full of them.

I tried to laugh it off for a while — how absurd I was being — but the heartbreak was real. It was just misplaced. There were many heartbreaks, and many heartbreakers, and they all served the same purpose; if I was dwelling on the empty space beside me, and who might have filled it, then I was not thinking about anything else. I was not remembering worse traumas and illnesses and memories of death. I was escaping specific fears by living in a perpetual state of anxiety. *Why has he not called? Why does he not want me? Why has he left?* Not: *Why did that happen? How did he die? When will he die? What will I do?* Those were the real heartbreakers. But I blamed all the palpitations, the shortness of breath, the dizziness, on whoever I had most recently met, whichever latest man would play the role, this repetitive walk-on part that my subconscious despair had so expertly directed.

I moved apartments in the summer, when my flatmates told me I was not allowed to make coffee on weekends before twelve, in case I should wake them. So I gave up that view of the Sacré-Coeur — the only real benefit of that flat-share — and the tiny single bed, and moved to a rougher, but more relaxed part of town, over the hill. The kids broke up for the summer, around then, and I found myself with very little to do. I had no purpose for every day anymore, nothing to keep me grounded, with the daily routine of my job gone. I had little money; I was living on what I had saved up in advance. The man I had been entranced by had left the city. He was not merely emotionally unavailable but logistically impossible, too.

To distract myself from the newly expanded void, I went on more dates, but nothing ever worked out. I didn't really want them to. I stopped giving out my number or making any plans, as the weeks dragged on. Everything in Paris was pastel but I was still navy, indigo, deepening and emptying each day, oblivious to the summer outside of myself. I couldn't forget what I wanted to forget — could not absolve myself of the diffuse fear that clung to my every movement. I became so exhausted by the burden of it that one day I just switched off, got sick and surrendered.

I couldn't get out of bed, then. It was as if standing was falling, pointless even to attempt. I stayed there so long that the details of my room began to taunt me. The skulls on my navy scarf, fading in the light by the window. Teeth chattering and migraine sickness, cigarette nausea and weak tea. Lilac nail polish — the only sympathetic smell, it seemed, then. Respite from swirling pain, confused nostalgia, those fevered visions. Could I find such peace in a walk around the block, a tiny little bath, a Nespresso pod?

I entertained these thoughts, these actions, but I continued to not get up. I stayed in the old-fashioned bed, in the old-fashioned room, with old-fashioned rose-pink wallpaper that I liked very much, certainly more than getting out of bed. I was happy enough here, I thought at first. This would do, this pretty Parisian cell. It would do until I was forced out of bed by hunger, at least.

When at last I was hungry enough to get up, I put on some clothes and went down the street to the supermarket. I had always disliked supermarkets, to the point where I wondered if I had a phobia of them: the glaring white strip lights and too many items and decisions to make. Things I wanted and things I couldn't really afford or were too unhealthy, or had something that I may or may not have been allergic to. All the everyday, futile little problems that I exaggerated and hated at once. They didn't even need to be problems: I had made them into problems. It was entirely my fault that I was wandering around a French supermarket wanting to die.

Eventually I picked up things that I needed: milk, coffee, wine, bread, some vegetables and fruit. I felt sick of these things upon buying them. The idea of having to cook anything filled me with dread. I was hungry but couldn't really imagine eating. I passed the flowers, suffocated in cellophane, hanging by the side of an aisle, wilting incrementally.

I reached the checkout and spoke minimal French. I had once enjoyed the challenge of improving my French, but now it was one more handicap. I piled the foods into a canvas shopping bag and paid the money and smiled and left. I felt desperately inadequate. I was hungry but then I was sick. And if I could be sick and bored here, in Paris, then there was no hope. If all I wanted to do was stare at the wallpaper and lie in the bath, and even then, I was still miserable, then something must be wrong. Paris had always been a good escape, the best escape of them all. But now, here I was, wanting out. Anything would do; I thought of options that would be easy, things in pill form.

There were no painkillers, though, and no people to bring them. It always takes sickness to realise you're alone. Voices in the music, matching my own regret — but why? How could I try any harder? How could I stop my heart aching for no apparent reason? Where did my flatmate keep her Valium? She had talked about her breakdowns and the tablets for emergencies; this seemed to measure up. I'd fit her size.

I'd manage two. The panic dragged on and then dissolved into fatigue, headaches, with wound-up thoughts and vague dreams. Fantasies, scratched down with good intentions. Quickly, it came to that.

I found the Valium, eventually, in a little white bottle. The language of languages, medical terms. Drug names. *Diazepam* in any country. I walked into a dream, where I did not feel guilty, for once, for not leaving my bed. I did not feel ashamed for being still. The jarring angst and neglect of my childhood drifted away; in some ways, I felt more myself than before.

Even with the medication, though, which was inevitably fleeting, the depression and paralysing anxiety persisted, as did my drab romanticism. But heartbreak was easier to dwell on than the idea that perhaps I needed professional help, and I convinced myself that this was what I was suffering from. It was more accessible a problem, in a way, more obvious, easier to rationalise. Heartbreak always had a solution, too, which other problems seemed not to. With heartbreak, the solution was simply that, at some point, I would meet someone else. However much I indulged one loss, I knew there were others out there, more numbers to call, glances to meet, ways to escape. They would be drawn to me too, those who needed to escape, the sailors looking out for the sirens.

I was happy when I found one. Having someone next to me would help alleviate all the anxiety and terror for a while. In the early days of a relationship, I'd sleep soundly, blissful and content. I would feel safe in another's arms, and in the heady distraction of new love, or infatuation — the joy of possibility. This was life; love was life. Love was the only thing that could possibly defy the pain of illness and grief.

And yet just as death is part of life, loss and decay are also part of love. And so whenever love became complicated, threatened to dissipate or disappear, the Fear returned. I could not stand the lows, and yet I persisted anyway. I was stubborn as any addict. I could not let up. I would not surrender. These love affairs were my only way out, it seemed to me. They were the only thing that could ward against those other demons. I set the new demons against the old ones, reactively.

In so doing, I evaded the root causes, the original traumas and neglect — a sick father, an ex-boyfriend who had overdosed on crack and heroin the year before, a traumatic, abusive relationship at university, and a rape a few years before that. I focused instead on the immense emptiness I felt in this particular moment, or whenever my supply of fleeting romance had run out. I focused on how nothing else worked, how nothing could take the edge off the abyss of unresolved terror that I had sought so stubbornly to repress. Nothing worked the way love did, or what I thought could be love. I was shameless in the hopelessness of this romanticism, which I was also aware of, and even addicted to. It bordered on nihilistic, really, but I didn't care. It was the mood I was in. Men had caused me such pain and such terror in the past, and now I sought out new men, as if their masculinity could shield me from the terror of my past, and the more casual threats of men standing too close in bars, or walking nearby in badly lit streets, being lecherous on the bus. I wanted to be protected, as if having a dangerous dog might protect me against the other dangerous dogs. They could be loyal sometimes. With this borrowed masculinity, these fleeting protectors, I could negotiate what and whom I was afraid of — unless they turned on me, that is. It was always a shock, despite these patterns, to realise I was sleeping with the enemy.

As the summer went on, I floundered on in this state of anxiety and fearfulness, feeling heartbroken. I became horizontal, and yet alone — closed off, somewhere between disassociation and delirium. I was always sad. At a loss, I began to write depressing little notes to myself, longing for a non-existent romance, ignoring everything and everyone else that might have hurt me. Love to stop the ground from swelling, revealing itself as the sea beneath my toes — that was the ideal, the solution, the cure.

Gradually, as the days went on, I forgot the symptoms, the shakiness. I blamed myself for what had come over me. I called it names now, other than heartbreak: depression, anxiety, PTSD — as if labelling could cure by means of compartmentalisation alone. I opened my arms to an emptiness that I could not contain; I surrendered further, but only because I was sure it was only a matter of time until I would have a better cure, again. Love was still the cure, even if it was not the only disease. I was determined that must be the case. *Love*, from a record, too much love, packed away and dusty. Something to want and want and want and leave, some day. Because in the end, did I really want love, or did I want to mourn its end, its failure? Love was death. I knew that. These men were not supposed to stick around; that was the point. Deep down, I'm sure, the idea of them sticking around forever was more terrifying than them leaving. How could I be so heartbroken, then? I would have to get upset at the original loss, the deeper fears.

I missed my father, for instance, but I was loathe to admit that. He had been sick with cancer for eighteen years, and he was always on the verge of death, and yet just as he had denied his condition for so long, I had grown up practising some performance of denial, too. He was always going, in a way, and I was used to that, but in recent months I had felt the need to go back to him. Without the children to babysit,

I became a child again myself. I had no one to look after but myself, and I couldn't do it alone. And so the wounds opened up. I wanted to go home as much as I wanted to be free of it. There were so many associations, most of them bad. I knew he could not look after me, that I would end up looking after him instead, but regardless this need to return nagged at me.

The insomnia and anxiety and panic attacks did not subside, and the need to go home grew stronger as the weeks went on. I would lie awake, my mind racing with hauntings I could not untangle from the very fibre of my consciousness. I was in a spiral of anxiety and fearfulness. In the city of Sartre and De Beauvoir, the existential crises and tortured dynamics they had written about were evident and all too present, timeless and clinging. I was bored, I was anxious, and I was confused, and they had been here, too, of course.

Though I had moved to Paris with some optimism, despite the months that preceded the move, before long I had found myself languishing in this barely repressed despair, lacking meaning, structure and any sense of security. It should not have been especially surprising that I might feel this way — a newly heartbroken philosophy graduate in Paris — and yet, somehow, it was. How could this city, this freedom, a fresh start, not liberate me? Why could I not, after everything, escape my own past and the neuroses that had found their way into my thoughts and reactions? Had I learned nothing at all from my degree? I had written a dissertation on Nietzsche's denouncement of the slave mentality, and the pursuit of life as a "free spirit". I had written an exam paper defending a life of artistic freedom and decadence; I had written about radical feminism and liberation from the shackles of the patriarchy. And yet here I was, in some ways very free, but still emotionally trapped, unable to enjoy whatever freedoms I had fought for and found. Fear was everywhere; I could not escape.

So now what? Nothing I did made any difference. I was stuck in this fearfulness every day and every night. Therapy? I could barely bring myself to talk. Medication? I had not reacted to it well in the past (other than the sort I would not be prescribed for any length of time). I had some sense that I needed to figure things out on my own, in an intellectual and emotional way, or any other solution would collapse eventually.

I wanted to know what the Fear, manifesting as this present mood, meant, and why it affected my entire perception of the world around me — from how I looked at my bedroom walls to how I approached relationships and engaged with people on a daily basis. Sartre, following Heidegger, had written about fear as an ontological field, the way in which we understood reality, and therefore built into the structure of being. Fear, like anxiety and boredom, was a state in which we all lived and understood life. "Emotions, moods, sentiments, and feelings are not accidents of human existence," as Lauren Freeman and Andreas Elpidorou write about their work, "they do not happen to us. Rather, we exist the way we do because of and through our affective experiences."[2] According to Heidegger, emotions are fundamental to human existence and define our realities and interactions; we are "mooded" beings. He created a system to understand these moods, this "moodedness", furthermore, and this involved separating fear, anxiety, and boredom, particularly, into clearly distinct categories, where

---

2   Freeman, Lauren and Elpidorou, Andreas, 'Fear, Anxiety and Boredom,' in *The Routledge Handbook of Phenomenology of Emotions*, ed. T. Szanto & H. Landweer. New York: Routledge, 2020.

anxiety and boredom were "fundamental moods" and fear, though entwined with anxiety, less important in terms of understanding the development of human nature itself. In fact, he saw fear as undermining of human nature and one's own growth and understanding of it. Anxiety and boredom, however, could become the fertile ground for personal growth in a deeper sense.

The mood I was in seemed to me to be a combination of all three of these states, however — there were at once immediate fears, diffuse anxiety, and a sort of disassociated numbness and disillusionment that felt like boredom and resonated with Heidegger and then Sartre's descriptions of what they meant by that alienated state. These moods were all entangled, though, and I didn't think they could be so neatly defined and detached from one another as Heidegger had argued.

As I understood and experienced it, what seemed at first a sort of diffuse anxiety was often a result of *remembering* immediate threats and traumatic events, and finding the sense of fear reverberating through my mind and body anarchically. This makes sense, when you consider that post-traumatic stress disorder is characterised by the reliving of traumatic events, often through flashbacks, and living *as if* the threat is still somehow immediate, or a similar threat may be. So although the threat was not actually, physically immediate, it felt as if it were, when the past encroached on the present in the intense way that it did. The anxiety I experienced was therefore not without a specific focus or fear, in this state of post-traumatic stress, even though, in reality, there was no longer that threat. Through the reliving of traumatic memories, despite attempts to suppress them, this state between fear and anxiety, which I have termed the Fear, emerged, blurring the past threats with present mood, revealing them to be entangled rather than distinct.

Likewise, boredom — experienced as a sort of numbness and listlessness, rooted in a realisation of profound meaninglessness, according to Sartre[3] — could also be experienced as part of a traumatised state — and especially the impossibility of coming to terms with events that seemed senseless and illogical, whose meaning or value escaped me. For me, fear was one part of a state of mind that also involved anxiety and boredom, or numbness, and a crisis of finding any meaning or value in present life, as well as past experiences. They were not, as Sartre and Heidegger had written, always moods that could be meaningfully detached from one another, but in my own experience, they were profoundly entangled and impossible to fully understand apart. They were also, importantly, a consequence of trauma and oppression, and reactions to wider political and social realities; the Fear, as I understood it, was the mind and body crying out for a different reality altogether. It was political and spiritual as well as psychological. It was an existential crisis, spilling into each of these spheres and relevant to all of them.

Emotion in a general sense, according to Sartre, existed as a reaction to insurmountable problems, which seemed impossible to solve or survive through pragmatism alone. Emotion was a way of escaping reality, in our minds, as a reaction to this sense of impossibility. It was ultimately a transformative process, a beginning of action that could change reality itself.

We take refuge in unconsciousness and disassociation, in switching off, in retreating from the world, even as we yearn for

---

3   Ibid.

something better. Emotion, in itself, is a way of transforming our own consciousness, of briefly denying reality. Fear, then, also removes us from reality when it is too difficult to cope with, when the threats are so severe, through various triggered responses, from fainting to running to disassociating. But "it is magical, so its power is limited". The threat may not exist "in our world"[4] when one is detached from reality through an emotional response, but it still exists, and the natural emotional response can therefore complicate the realistic escape from threat.

This helps explain why addiction is so difficult either to live with or to attempt to alleviate in others; it is predicated on this natural response to threat, which is to remove oneself from reality. It is a stress response that constitutes our perception of the world and other people, our understanding of what we need and what we don't. In a moment of pain and terror, even if that experience has been partly caused by a drug, or a bad relationship, or grief, the natural instinct — in everyone, but especially so for an addict — is to escape, to switch off, as if life depended on it. The sad irony of course is that this "magical thinking" is illogical, and while in the immediate situation "solves" the problem of the threat, in the sense that we can no longer feel the terror of it and can remove it from our minds, it has not actually gone. We have simply anaesthetised ourselves to our realities, looked the other way, deluded ourselves. And then, in the morning, the Fear returns, more intensely than before.

Addiction is one of the most obvious examples of this fight or flight (or freeze) response, and indicative of how this instinct itself constitutes reality (since it triggers more such responses,

4   Ibid.

more fear, more flight, since it can alter one's entire life). There are also parallels with other reactive emotional behaviours, such as becoming romantically or sexually obsessed (rather than face one's own traumas), or any number of activities and ways of thinking that remove us from the immediate situation that we are struggling with. What is significant is that the reaction itself changes our realities, and not typically for the better, in the longer term; the original problem doesn't go away, but simply becomes more complex, and our reactions to it often deepen this.

"The Fear", as I experienced it, was a state of mind that affected how I felt physically, how I experienced everyday life, and how I perceived and engaged with others and the world around me, whenever my latest escape had dissolved. My worldview was characterised by shutting down, panicking, dissociating and running away. It was characterised by escapism, one way or another, because the reality of my current life — overwhelmed as it was by past traumas and betrayals, stretching so many years back, much of it suppressed — felt impossible at that time. It was too heart-breaking to stay present in, so I ran from one escape strategy to another until I simply burnt out. And then I began again.

Though it did not feel very meaningful at the time — rather something to endure and then also escape — my experience of this state ultimately taught me a lot about my own existence, how my mind and body worked, and about human nature in a broader sense. The Fear defined how I lived; it was an affective experience that also revealed to me how existence itself was characterised and infused with such states and their manifestations as moods and reactions and relationships with each other. The Fear felt like an ordeal, and it was, but it was also central to human existence, I came to realise, and it transformed my own understanding of the world and our emotionally rooted place in it. I realised I would never understand human nature without coming to terms with my own version of the Fear — these entangled states of fear, anxiety and boredom — and I would never emerge beyond these emotional states myself without understanding the nature of this state, and how it changed and changes me and others everywhere.

After the peak of that particular breakdown, in which I realised how I might eventually recover, I decided to leave Paris, and with it the escape it had promised, and yet which I realised could only ever be fleeting and superficial. I enrolled in a Masters in Terrorism Studies, affordable only because it was close to home. I had been scared all the time — so what better to study than terrorism? I would analyse the modern folk devil. The face of evil. Terror itself. An entire war, which had shadowed, and defined, the era I had grown up in, had been a war on an *emotion*, after all, and more than that, a war justified by emotion.

So I signed myself up, not so much to wage war on the emotion, as our governments were so determined to, but to understand the emotion that seemed to define the entire world and its actions at this point. What was this terror? How and why did it usurp our lives and sense so dramatically? Was my terror somehow related to the one that my country had waged a war on, too? And where better to study it than my childhood home, with my father dying in the next room? In the same place I had once fled to after a life-changing assault? What better way to face my fears than to move right in with them? The abyss beckoned, and once again — perhaps unwisely — I dived straight in.

Thus began an exploration, which would take almost a

decade, into terror, anxiety, reactive behaviours, and the fearful emotional state at its heart. I wanted to understand the mindset — and physical state of which it was part — that would so often define not simply how I lived, but how I perceived the world around me, and the people around me — which would determine the decisions I made and the memories that would linger, the relationships that would develop and how they would dissolve. This mindset, moreover, defined the world we lived in, and the politics that pushed it one way or another.

The book that follows now is the culmination of those years — those experiences, studies and ideas — and an attempt, ultimately, to understand what this particular state of mind reveals about human existence and spirit itself, and how it defines the world around us and the political struggles under the surface. I wanted to understand the Fear in order to escape it, initially; this book is a story about my attempts to confront, deconstruct and evade this force, this emotion, this spectre, this mood — at times to surrender to it, and ultimately to learn to live with and, sometimes, transcend it. It has taught me, more crucially, about the psychological and emotional repression and oppression that defines our world and keeps us in perplexing and at times tortuous cycles of behaviour, on individual and collectives scales.

Although it took many years to wrestle with this demon — the demon of demons — I learnt in some way to love and appreciate its darkness, and what it revealed in myself and others, as gradually I laid it to rest, and transcended into a more optimistic mindset and political spirit.

In Love and War

It was mid-September when I first arrived back to Fife to begin my Masters. I grew up with my sisters on the coast, in a cottage in the woods. It seemed idyllic at times, with the animals and ancient trees, the stories of pagan rituals and our ancestors' part in them centuries ago. Apparently the woods had once been a haven for women accused of witchcraft, during the 1600s, and they would dance around fires together. Before that, another ancestor was shot in the back, while on horseback, defending his own prisoner, whom he had taken hostage as part of a plot to defend Mary Queen of Scots. He was so loyal to Mary, apparently, that would rather die than give up the hostage — ultimately not perhaps the wisest move in a personal sense. My father liked to tell these stories, anyway, the very old stories. He said less about his own recent past, though.

As it turned out, he had lived a very interesting life before we came around. There were rumours he had been some sort of clandestine diplomat, some sort of spy, even, but he never commented on any of these suggestions with anything other than an evasive laugh. He had served in Berlin during the height of the Cold War, I found out later on, for instance, where he smuggled friends from East Berlin to West in the boot of his car. After that, he turned down an invitation to join the SAS, instead becoming an architect and editor. But then, in the late 80s and early 90s, when my sisters and I were born, he was often away — in Finland and Russia, it turned out. He led a diplomatic effort to save Alvar Aalto's Viipuri Library from destruction after it was taken over by the Russians, but we only found out about this when he was given a Knighthood by the Finnish government for "Services to Architecture." It seemed that there was a bit more to the story than architecture, but nevertheless, I never found out much more than these details; no matter how many times I subtly asked him, he would not tell. He barely spoke at all about his former life.

Current issues had eclipsed the past, anyway; when I was eight, he was diagnosed with Stage Four kidney cancer. Though he somehow managed to survive another 18 years of sickness, the strains of his illness as well as previous unwise financial decisions meant that everything became run-down, and even the stories, whenever he chose to tell them, seemed tired. There had been this former life of glamour and intrigue, but we were part of the new life, which was markedly different, and in many ways bore the brunt of that past life. So here we were, living far from anyone else: three sisters sharing a small bedroom and baths, with a father who barely spoke (and certainly not of the war), with our mother, in the woods. People had looked at us strangely, and avoided the woods, too.

Now the leaves on the trees at home were beginning to turn shades of yellow, ochre and peach, yet to fall and cover the grass in the woods and the lawns in mounds. The days were still long enough, with the evening hours stretching out in the pinks, fluorescent oranges and deep greys of sunset. The sea glimmered peacefully on the horizon, beyond the barleyfields, where a family of deer would tentatively and gracefully roam around in the mornings, nibbling the crops for food. Overhead, there were rooks, blackbirds and often hawks, their vast wings outstretching as they embarked on another flight, later settling back in the ancient trees.

Why had people been afraid of this place? The crowd of crows in the trees did not scare me, because I had grown up with them and barely noticed the raucous noise whenever someone walked by. The old superstitions did not affect me because these birds comforted me, were of the present and the recent past, real things, rather than the symbols of old mythologies and superstitions. Familiarity bred attachment, in my case. I would always associate crows with home, before death, although, looking back, I associated home with death, too. It, and the crows, had always been there. Perhaps because my family, by living there, were at the mercy of nature to such an extent — living surrounded by trees that would threaten to fall on the house during the many strong gales — death, like the crows, seemed merely a part of this natural wilderness, a sort of everyday warning signal, a quotidian threat. Locals avoided the woods, and yet for me that made it more special, more of a refuge, and more peaceful. This eerie, windswept place was my home; the crows were cohabitants, raising the alarm if anyone came close to intruding on it. I felt lucky for that, as if I were in on their secret, too.

I was glad to be back anyway, and this summer more than any time I had been back before. Though I had been racked with anxiety before, now I was only relieved I had made the decision to come home; it felt right on a deep, subconscious level, to be there again, despite everything that had worried me about it before. I enjoyed the cool breeze from the North Sea and the total absence of city pollution; being in the woods again, walking in between the tall elms and beeches, felt like a process of renewal, of purifying the toxins of the city and its closed-in rooms. My anxiety lessened further as I took comfort in preparing for the new academic year, safe in a familiar routine and other people's orders.

The School of International Relations was on the Scores in St Andrews, a street by the edge of a cliff face which overlooked East Sands beach, and a few minutes away from where we had lived when I was younger. It was also where my father's grandparents had once lived, and he had grown up swimming in the open-air pool as a child. I had also swum in the sea, a little further down, on the beach, trying to delude myself it was warm, that I was in a sunnier climate, until the numbness set in and I felt no more cold. This was how we had both grown up, in a way — delusion and then numbness. *Hardiness.* Endurance tests encouraged by those around us, by our families and even by the weather itself.

I didn't swim in the sea anymore, but I could see it from the Centre for the Study of Terrorism and Political Violence, a little section of the School with only a few offices. It was known as a "retirement program for former spies", according to one PhD student, and this was not really an exaggeration. There were, however, regular academics as well, specialising in subjects from Hamas to modern piracy to the IRA and the far-right.

The Masters intake was quite small — there were only eight of us. There were a few Americans, a couple of Eastern Europeans and two Scots (myself included). There were also people on the distance learning version of the course who would sit in virtually; one of them insisted on disguising himself with his own shadow for every single seminar, which we had to pretend was normal.

Quite early on, my interests diverted from the mainstream subjects to Critical Terrorism Studies; I was interested in State Terrorism and the media's framing of political violence. To what extent was the terrorist threat exaggerated, and how did it cause a rise in Islamophobia? How was torture framed to seem more effective and ethical than it actually was? How did the media manipulate the public into supporting wars that were neverending and mislead, through the heightening of anxiety and mass panic? What was the real threat to us all? Why were we so afraid? Did the societal fear of the terrorist mask a deeper, repressed fear, as my own fear of abandonment by random men had also concealed my deeper traumas?

—

Both of my parents were at home at first, but my mother had to go to London for work for a few weeks, shortly after term started. She had rarely been able to go away by herself as my father had not really been well enough to be alone for any period of time. He had had seizures over the years and because we lived in the countryside, it wouldn't have been sensible to leave him for too long. Now that I was back, though, she took her opportunity.

At first it was an enjoyable time, and quite a rare experience, to be alone with my father. I had barely spoken to him on his own in years, partly because he rarely spoke at all, but also because when my mother was there he seemed to keep to himself far more, as if his bedroom was a bunker. He tended to stay in his bed, reading and writing and watching the news. Entire weeks would pass with nothing more than the occasional "Morning", "Coffee?" or "Good night". He was an enigma to me, almost a mute, though he could be charming and social amongst other people, out of the bunker. This contradiction caused feelings of rejection when I was younger; I heard stories about him, but not from him. I asked questions but got no answers. I did not understand why he was so remote and secluded, as if his very existence depended on being disassociated from family life entirely.

My mother explained that his own mother's death, when he was four, had traumatised him, but little else was said that would explain either that or the silence that followed (and had predated the cancer). The subject was off bounds, especially with him. I only knew that she had died of an overdose at twenty-six, towards the end of the Second World War, while her husband was fighting in Monte Cassino, Italy. My father was swiftly sent off to boarding school after her death. He was not allowed to grieve or heal; he was permitted only to be seen but not heard — a generational curse, and one that continued into adulthood.

What he did do, however, as the years went on, was read and watch films. As his cancer progressed, these forms of escapism, or healing, became ever more pronounced and necessary. For me, conversely, his ever-more imminent death inspired a need to find more physical distance. I had sought to free myself from the heavy, unspoken despair that clung to my father's every movement and mannerism, the secrets he would not share and the spectre of death he seemed to embody. He may have found reading therapeutic, but the lack of familial communication, the closed-off life, stirred only rejection and fear in me. He left, emotionally, and was fading away physically, so I reacted by escaping the despair this caused in every way I could. And yet Paris had not worked out, nothing and nowhere else had either. As the years had gone on, the desire to know him better had never left. And so here, finally, we were living together, just us, alone, for the first time in my entire life, with no one to divide or distract us.

He seemed happy at first, sitting in the evening, as usual,

with rows of books behind him and the news on and the wind picking up outside, beyond the shuttered windows. As the days went by, though, his moods worsened, as did his symptoms, and I began remembering all the times I had fleetingly been home before, and why I had left, and why I had felt a mixture of guilt and relief. I began cleaning up after him a lot; it took up more and more time. He would leave a trail of petty destruction behind him: piles of dirty dishes from various messy snacks, a dirty bathroom that he had no intention of cleaning, and which at times seemed intentional, vindictive even. Cheese smeared on the rails of the fridge. It was as if he were a toddler having a tantrum, but he was somehow less direct about it. He would not tell me anything was wrong, only desecrate the shared environment.

He would shout at animals as well, and occasionally a passing walker if they came too close to the house or if he was in the wrong mood. I would get woken up in the night from his screaming — from nightmares, it turned out — or later on, at dawn, from his hacking cough, that never ever cleared up. Some mornings I would wake to the sound of vomiting. I would see him writing letters to people, in his particular tiny handwriting, realising that the act of it made him happier.

He had become very frail by this point, finding it hard to walk since the cancer had spread to his bones some years ago. Sometimes he did not need a stick, at least at home, but on painful days, or when it was particularly cold, he would take one of about twenty wooden sticks if he needed to move around. He would stay in bed often, as time went on. He had suffered a broken spine a couple of years ago, during a seizure, which he had initially tried to pass off as a mere ache. Since then, mobility had become more of an issue.

Despite the everyday difficulties of living with him, that

time with my dad was ultimately an illumination of how hard his life was, and how well he coped, day in and day out. I also realised how scared he was, which had never occurred to me before, because he had always seemed the image of strength and stoicism. He seemed, even in his worst periods, beyond fear, and yet now I realised that fear overshadowed his life on every level. How could it not? He was scared of dying, he was scared of losing his mind, he was scared of falling, scared of being shown up, embarrassed, weak, dependent. He was scared of his own past, and scared of the future. He was scared of the disease that was gradually taking him away from what he loved — his physical freedom, taking over his own body and mind and the everyday details and routines he cherished. He was always living with fear. He was always fighting against it.

I had not realised before, either, how much I had also lived with that fear, how I had grown up under this spectre of anxiety, panic and sometimes sheer terror. I had absorbed his fear, and it had bled into my own. I had shrunk away from myself to accommodate this cancer and the darkness it perpetuated. I had barely known myself, at times, in this effort merely to survive and keep up the appearances that would help him survive, too. I couldn't let the side down, could not admit to the terror that subsumed us all.

We were always waiting for this death, this unknown, amorphous thing. Always worried, never settled. Constant flight or fight (mostly flight). My father had been brought up to avoid emotion, for emotion was seen as a sign of weakness, and so he suffered in silence. But I could and had always seen and felt his suffering and his fear, and I had absorbed it as my own. The Fear was contagious, and my heart broke for him, and even as I pushed the thoughts away, that for a long time

I had been eclipsed by this disease, which rotted everything in its path and paralysed any sense of true joy, I clung to it because I clung to him.

In those weeks and months, as these things became apparent to me more consciously, we became closer. There were no long conversations or soul searching. I simply lived alongside him for a while and helped when I could and tried to make him feel comfortable and unselfconscious. While sometimes I would wonder if his more difficult behaviour was intentional or cruel, I gave him the benefit of the doubt. He was not a saint, but then he didn't have to be. He was ill but he was proud and sometimes his condition frustrated him. Sometimes a mood took over, or memory loss would dismay him, or the small details of life would become unbearably confusing. Nightmares plagued him and claustrophobia tied him to his thoughts. He missed being younger and mobile. He missed being able to book a flight and get away. He missed the years of compulsive travel and independence, keeping secrets, being impossible to track down. He missed being able to run, to escape. He missed exhilaration. He feared death, and loss, and losing his mind. He feared his own past. He seemed strong in many ways, but he was haunted.

I could not sleep either. His fears and frustrations kept me up at night, too.

———

Later in the year, when my mother was away on a different trip, and he came out of his shell again, he offered to drive me into St Andrews for my tutorial, while he would have some lunch at a café. The class was on terrorism and the Internet, about the use of Internet forums for recruitment and propaganda and the idea of "cyber-terrorism". We were talking about whether it was a real threat or not, when I realised I had several missed calls and a voicemail from an unknown number, and then a text message. It said that my dad had fallen in the street and needed to be picked up and taken to the doctor. I asked if I could be excused.

He was being looked after by a shoe shop manager, near where he had fallen. He was smiling when I arrived, and acting like nothing was wrong, as if he was just having a charming conversation with a new acquaintance. But as the shop manager told me, he had actually fallen quite badly. "He'll need stitches", she said. "If he lets you see, he's hurt his head." He had covered his new wound with a hat.

He had been blown over in the strong gales. He laughed it off and said that everything was fine, despite the deep cut on his forehead and the bruising around his nose. The trick with him was to go along with this, but to just subtly insist on going home via the doctor, as it was near the supermarket anyway, and we needed something for dinner. The best thing was to make sure it was all very matter of fact and not dramatic. So we went to the minor injuries clinic, and waited there calmly. I told him I would go over to the supermarket and pick up a couple things while he waited. Outside, in the wind, I realised I was shaken, too, but I kept walking briskly and picked up everything I thought he needed, something he would like for dinner, if he was feeling better. I took his lead, to take the lead.

When I went back into the hospital, the nurse's door was open and I could see him being stitched up. The nurse finished up as I was there, giving us some instructions. He smiled in his kind way and was very polite and charming. We went back to the car. I told him about what I had bought him for dinner.

At home, he went to bed, and I put the oven on. I brought

him dinner on a tray, and he was still very sweet and polite. He watched the news, the rest of the world going through their traumas as the gales continued to blow outside in the woods.

There was so much about him that I didn't know, and I realised this acutely in those weeks we were together. I started asking more questions, saying I was practising interview techniques for my course, but he would provide only the vaguest and shortest of answers, a smile and a slight, evasive laugh whenever I tried. After a while I gave up asking, knowing it was futile. Instead, I started cooking for him more, especially when he was ill. I cooked him breakfast every morning — poached eggs — and we would eat together and drink coffee.

He began to reciprocate. He would offer me whiskey in the evening, as the sun set over the expansive fields and the long grasses in the woods. One day in the late spring he surprised me by bringing home a whole lobster from the local harbour, just because it was a sunny day. In these moments, he seemed better and happy, and we could just be father and daughter for once. He smiled, sitting in the garden, the sun in his face. He read the newspaper, as the birds darted around, on the edge of the woods. I lay down on the lawn, the happiest I had ever been, and seeing him the happiest I had ever seen him.

And yet, outside of these moments, in which we could be victorious for a little while, delight in the hours together and forget the ever-present illness, the Fear would return and shadow over our relationship, our lives — for him, of course, far more so than for me. But I became fearful in a general sense, absorbing his own terror, and mourning his loss pre-emptively. Surely, that was my real threat, the real fear? I was studying terrorism, but for me the greatest terrorism, for many years, was my father's cancer and all that went with it. The fear was that he would die. I didn't know when, but it would be soon. The threat was always there. It stopped me living fully; it paralysed me into a sense of waiting, nervously. Death loomed over me, always.

Had I misplaced my fear of his death onto this wider, societal threat? Had I projected my fear of abandonment onto random men who flitted in and out of my life? Why was it so hard to stare at it directly, to mourn it? Why did I end up in this strange, circular mindset, where I could see death and terror everywhere except in my moments with him? It was almost as if I was so desperate to shield the time that we had left that I delegated the fearfulness of his death to other things.

And so I deflected from the real threats in my life by taking on many others instead — living like a thrill-seeker at times, never fully believing that there was anything beyond the moment, but also haunted by the realities I was suppressing or avoiding.

He was going to die soon, but I didn't want to think about that, so I filled my days, when not merely being reckless or scattered like I had been before, with lectures on terrorist attacks, propaganda, heightened threat levels and the culture of fear that perpetuated this communal mindset.

I saw fear everywhere, and I was not wrong to. My own experiences revealed to me that this misplaced fearfulness was endemic and defined not only the way in which we lived as individuals, but as societies. Was I compartmentalising, deflecting and projecting by doing all of this? Absolutely. But it turned out to be a useful practice, or at least an enlightening one. My poison was a common one.

—

In Terrorism Studies tutorials, we learned less about the specific emotions of fear and anxiety, and more about their practical, political consequences. We learnt about security and threat, insecurity and action. We learnt about self-defence, protection and "pre-emptive war". I learnt a new language of justification and framing — the public relations of global politics. Inevitably, I learnt about its hypocrisy, about the cynicism and nihilism of *realpolitk*. I learnt about the bizarre desire to "conquer hearts and minds" with new media and with drone strikes, with narratives of saving and protecting. I learnt about "shock and awe", both planned and leaked, public and private. I learnt about masculinity, more than anything, ever more familiar with this immense, shaky bravado around which the world seemed to spin.

What fascinated me most, though, was how terrorism is as much about the spectacle as it is about fear itself; the shock accentuates the original fear, which is concerned with death, injury and loss. It is precisely the element of surprise that is so disarming and effective in exaggerating already formidable concerns. Psychological warfare involves forcing a *perpetual* fearfulness, a constant state of instability and doubt, a rattling of one's sense of safety and self. It is this feeling, or rather this extended existential state, that had consumed me in Paris and for many years before that, and which fascinated me now.

What had once closed in on me in a personal crisis now became a subject outside of myself, a phenomenon relevant the world over. I thought there must be value in knowing more about this state — the Fear, in a wider sense — its diameters, its causes and effects, its various manifestations in the world at large. Though I had withdrawn from the world, and still felt a sense of alienation, the desire to study it brought me a little closer to others. This state of fearfulness was hardly an isolated experience, however much it felt so at the time. That was what was so fascinating about it: that you could feel so harrowingly alone in such a common human experience.

Terrorism, however, was also an explicitly social experience, with very communal, political consequences. It was a social crisis and the behaviour it inspired — mass mourning and ritualistic memorialisation, global wars — were, it seemed to me, a bizarre extrapolation and exaggeration of quite normal human emotions and behaviours. The Fear, whether in the context of terrorism or less public phenomena, is an emotional battlefield, in which threats, both real and imaginary, immediate and vague, coalesce into a state of mind that subsumes one's sense of self and strength. It is embodied and yet abstract, can be specific or diffuse. It is the process of being splintered and taken away from life, towards a personal abyss, a shadow of the self that is all-consuming and all-destructive.

Some find it in depression, some find it in addiction, some find it in the everyday, vampiric terror of abusive relationships. Some find it in the aftermath of trauma and illness. Some find it, as I have over the years, in all of these things, entangled and relentless and dragging. Some find it and cannot say why. Some may call it an existential crisis or a breakdown. Some will blame the state of the world for the state of their minds. This is often justified, at least partially. In our relationship with the world — with other people, places, substances, sensations and ideas — we are challenged not only to survive, but to understand our place within it, even (and especially) when we are at our most defeated. The Fear is about our own identity and the survival of everything that makes us recognisable to ourselves, in the face of forces that often seem intent on erasing that spirit or certainty, or so indifferent that disappearance is inevitable.

The Fear can be a challenge in a positive sense, as well as negative. It is not something merely to overcome, but to explore, to gain wisdom from. It is the dark side, our own shadow self — grasping at our consciousness, asking to be heard. The challenge is to listen, but not to succumb; to walk that line between accepting one's human weakness and accepting total defeat.

—

As the weeks and months went on, I read around the subject, from philosophy to psychoanalysis, from politics to anthropology. I wanted to understand how culture could inform and influence conceptions of threat levels, and the impact this had on every level of our lives and society. I wanted to reckon with the power held by myself and others in this context — the choices I had and did not have, and I observed and participated in the power and powerlessness of others.

And so, I began to explore my own personal fears — the things that had haunted me in my life to date, and the ways in which I had sought to escape their grip on me. I examined the loop between trauma, threat and continued anxiety, the way that shame, doubt and terror looped around one another, creating a short-circuited system, a flickering, anxious mind. I wanted to understand the personal and psychological implications of violence, in my own life and others', and the roots of it too — where fear is the currency of our actions and needs — and becomes so familiar that we think it is inevitable, the only conceivable way to live.

In love and war, and in fight and flight, we are at our most vulnerable, essential and perhaps most selfish. Ideals collapse beneath desperation. We may betray ourselves to survive; we may live miserably, out of love and the fear of losing it. We may become slaves to an emotion and a mental state and so, to one another. We may live as if we have already lost everything, unwittingly.

The Fear is a state of mind — a mode of perpetual flight or fight, of endless insecurity and escapism. I wanted to know why we were so afraid, and what we were afraid of. How did our responses to these fears shape our lives and wider societies? How was our political landscape defined by these fearful reactions? How did culturally constructed fears shape our everyday interactions?

I wanted to understand these things, and to piece together how fear itself defined not only individual actions but collective decisions. In moments of acute vulnerability, in the midst of this fear, who are we? Who was I? I had started this course because wanted to know how an emotional state could provoke violence, and how violence could cause an emotional state, and whether it was possible ever to escape this loop of reactivity and escapism and terror. I wanted, in the midst of all this, or perhaps even through this, to find some kind of peace.

States of Fear

Where there are people who are endemically fearful and reactive, it is not surprising that there will be politicised behaviours that operationalise, encourage and exploit this state of mind — and minds — for the acquisition of power. The capacity of humans to be scared leaves them vulnerable to subjugation; while fear can be a strength — in the sense that we have evolved this way to escape danger when it presents to us, with the complex interactions and dynamics of human societies — it also makes us easy prey and easy pawns. As I had realised in my own life, chronic fear could weaken me, physically and emotionally, as I sought to withdraw from the painful reality of the world, into something that felt fleetingly safer.

As I started writing essays on terrorism, state terrorism and civil wars, it became clear to me just how damaging chronic fearfulness could be on a societal level, and how it was typically exploited by those in power. What I found most interesting was how narratives of victimhood, shame and good-versus-evil were used in high-conflict situations to provoke and prepare for violence and strengthen ideas of community. To draw a community together — against another community — the "enemy" would be transformed into symbols of something feared — a threatening mass, monsters, rather than individual people. This would make it easier for one community to inflict or allow violence against the other, easier to render others powerless and worthless.

At the root of the state of fear, so often politicised, was this crucial power dynamic. It seemed to me futile to try to understand fear without analysing power and control and how they all intersected. Whether in my own personal life, or in wider political scenarios, fear and power were always entangled. I became fascinated by this dynamic, perhaps as a reaction to the strange relationship I had with fear myself; I felt powerless to it, and yet I wanted to have power over it, so I could be free from it. As I read about wars and propaganda, I could see these patterns of fear, powerlessness and the desire for control playing out over and over again. Fear itself was an experience of powerlessness, and it provoked myriad reactions — often the overplayed desire for power and actions that would facilitate that.

I thought back to the fight-or-flight concept, for instance. This is the mechanism by which a human body found a way, fleetingly, to control its consciousness and sense of reality, in reaction to a sense of panicked powerlessness, provoked by a perceived threat. When we cannot, in such a situation, transform our actual reality, we can transform our perception of it, our consciousness. At this primal level, we are wired to detach from reality as a way to have some control over it; a last-ditch attempt to survive. If we have no power, no sense of agency and consequence, then we might as well be dead. Survival is built around defeating this end; we live in fear that we will stop existing, and conversely, and at times even perversely, we disassociate, escape, deny and imagine our ways out of the terror of this eventuality.

As I learnt in lectures and readings, the terror of existential threat, both personal and national, individual and communal, also leads people to deny the existence of others, to dehumanise and to crush, if it means they can escape this existential terror. Whether provoked by a terrorist attack or an old trauma, the mechanism is the same. People fall into a blind rage or a fantasy or a drunken haze, if it means they will feel less close to death themselves. They will deny their neighbour's humanity if it means being surer of their own continued existence. A desire for survival, when people think that theirs is under attack (even if it is not), is enough to deny the reality of anyone else's.

This moment of panic, this situation where a person feels the need to defend their own existence, is often rationalised with stories. The basic and often ruthless instinct to defy fear of death is dressed up with narratives: virtuous victimhood, bravery in the face of adversity, good versus evil, civilisation versus barbarism. All of these stories are designed to articulate and order highly emotional situations that otherwise seem overwhelming and anarchic; they are also intended to define people's reactions to those events, to encourage a sense of catharsis, for instance, or a desire for vengeance, depending on the situation. These may or may not make any strategic sense, or have any ethical value, but have a certain emotional logic.

These stories become ideologies and philosophies and mythologies; our systems of living — political, religious, social — are rooted in the human tendency to tell stories after the fact. They are a way to affirm one's existence, or the existence of a nation or community or cause. We tell stories to keep living. Though sometimes these stories keep some people living at the expense of others.

—

The summer I was writing up my dissertation, I went to Derry for a conference on the Troubles called *Poisonous Legacies*. Whilst there, I met up with an Irish writer I'd met a few years earlier, when I was 21, who knew a lot about the Troubles himself. He had helpfully sent me some poems about the conflict, which I had shared with my class during my presentation on the IRA, in the hope of humanising "the other side" of the war. The seminar group were a mixture of students from Security Studies, Terrorism Studies and Peace and Conflict Studies; each had a different approach to political violence, ranging from military to psychological to diplomatic. It included a combination of future NGO workers, a drone operator, an American Air Force pilot and several who had their eyes on intelligence roles. Each group, anyway, could do with some help in understanding the perspective of the perpetrators of violence and their communities, and poetry became the best way I found to assist there.

During the weekend of the conference, I ended up staying with the writer and his family; the first thing his mother said was, "You are very welcome here". I had never felt so welcome anywhere in my life before, in fact; she was a kind and lovely person who immediately helped me feel settled and comforted, in a way that felt extremely rare and special.

Over the next few days, we attended the conference together, which was organised by the Pat Finucane Centre. We heard some recently declassified accounts of torture by the MoD. We heard from the victims' families. And then, when the hours of intense revelations were over, we'd drink together in the socialist bar, Sandino's, and discuss it all over again.

We started going out, soon after that. Later on, we'd joke that we were a product of the peace process. As the months and then years went on, this became a sadder joke, a rattling punchline, something that spoke to the reality of life after war — not quite war, and not quite peace.

At the beginning, we travelled between St Andrews and Derry, sometimes meeting in between, in Glasgow. I was offered a scholarship to stay on at St Andrews and do a PhD, on portrayals of terrorists in the media. He started writing a book about imaginary places; idealistic visions which never quite came true. Between the chapters, we drank together, in pubs by the sea or in Derry and Donegal, talking about our families and histories and all that we had inadvertently inherited. He told me about his father, and I told him about mine. We talked about people who had hurt us. We talked about wars. We drank whiskies — some Irish, some Scottish. When we were apart, we wrote new drafts of the chapters, new outlines, in mutual attempts to understand the dearth of destruction that preceded us.

"*Reactions to crisis and death, and the fear of death*", I wrote down in my notes as I started the PhD, apparently unaware that I was taking on this whole project, really, to be near my dying, mute, traumatised father — to try to understand him, and his fear, as well as my own. As if by exploring these issues on an intellectual level, I could understand him, know him, and fill in the absence I mourned without even realising it. As if by studying violence, I would eventually be freed from the trauma of it having been inflicted on me, too, when I was younger. I looked at all these pictures of terrorists by day, and tried to speak with my dad by night, but often, he looked the other way. Then I would phone my new boyfriend, and we'd talk about our projects, and again, our fathers, and again, these histories of violence. And for a while, it felt like progress.

As I started my new research, I looked at headlines that read "WANTED: DEAD OR ALIVE", images of crowds crying

and traumatised, accounts of underground searches for a
fallen dictator, not connecting any of this to my own father
issues, or that other trauma I had tried to block out — the
men, and a particular one man out there who had destroyed
me, but had never been found or convicted.

I looked at Bin Laden's disturbingly serene expression, his
draped gold and white clothes, his faraway eyes, and I could
see all of them and none of them — my demons, the men in
my life, those who terrorised me and then just disappeared.
I wanted to know their stories; this is what it had all come
down to. I wanted to understand their perspective, as well
as I could, to understand my own, and my culture, too, and
the ways in which these stories, these rituals, were rooted in
fear and the desire to overcome it and the desire, essentially,
to survive.

—

My father continued not to talk. But though he did not talk,
without even being aware of it, I started telling stories about
him, or at least writing them down. I started searching for his
story (when not researching "the story of terrorism"). I asked
my mother more questions, looking for answers he evaded —
about his mother, my grandmother, who had died at twenty-
six; about where they had lived; about where he had travelled
before he knew her, before I existed. By piecing together this
backstory he wouldn't tell, I tried, I think, to affirm the life of
a man not only about to die, but who had been emotionally
absent as long as I'd known him — a constant enigma. I
wanted to write him into existence. (I realise, writing this, I
still am, in some way; but also, more now than then, I write
myself back into existence, too.)

Stories are a survival instinct. We tell them to keep living, to be sure of our own perception, even when that perception is confused — to make thoughts "real". In wartime, we tell stories of brave heroes and virtuous victims, of babies born in bomb shelters and brave women singing to them by torchlight. We hear stories of people who fight to defend their country — in Ukraine, for example, most recently — when they have lost everything. We hear stories of those lives lost — the two elderly sisters, who had lived their whole lives together, executed by Russian soldiers, for no reason at all, other than that they were Ukrainian.[5] We hear and tell these stories to affirm their lives, to affirm their existence, when we know they should have lived, that they should still be there. We tell stories to deny and eventually to accept death. We tell stories when everything else feels hopeless.

In my thesis, I began looking at the stories we told about villains, about terrorists — Osama Bin Laden, Saddam Hussein, the Boston Bombers, among others. I researched witch hunts in the 1600s, Guy Fawkes, Abu Ghraib and lynching photographs. I traced the visual genealogies between them all, the ways in which political villains, regardless of guilt or innocence, have been portrayed over the centuries, and how ideas about ugliness, dirtiness, animals and "the Other" have sewn a thread through these times, retelling the same stories with the same features and symbols, over and over again, so that "playing the villain", a misogynistic, imperialist and racist project, has become tightly woven into Western culture: a story we are too familiar with.

The political villain is partially a made-up character.

---

5   Gall, Carlotta, 'Bucha's Month of Terror,' *The New York Times*, April 11, 2022

Although the perpetrators of political violence exist, those who become iconic and infamous are heavily mythologised, and in ways that link them together. Political villains may be vastly different in their political ideals, actions and identities, but when they become "iconic" they are turned into a stock character, more alike than not. Culture perpetuates this tradition and mythology, and the stereotypical ideas about evil and subversion, so that any political villain, elevated to this level of infamy, becomes demonic, a political Satan to the establishment's angels. Politics is entangled by notions of morality, and so political events become morality tales, always with the happy ending where the bad guy perishes. But politics is rarely quite so black and white. Nevertheless, the mythology persists, reducing complex political conflicts into tokenistic morality tales. These stories then become part of the fabric of our society, and whenever another villain takes the stage, we expect him or her to follow the same narrative, and to meet the same end.

In 1605, for instance, Guy Fawkes was accused of plotting to blow up the Houses of Parliament in a Catholic rebellion. Though there is some ambiguity about whether he did actually plot the attack, he was hung, drawn and quartered in front of a baying crowd for that crime regardless. Etchings and drawings of his punishment were produced to record the spectacle at the time, and children sang anti-Catholic songs every year since to celebrate his death. He was transformed into an effigy, which would be ritually burned on bonfires for the next few centuries, as a symbol of the defeat of his subversion. Later in the 1600s, the crazed persecution of witches spread all over Europe, from Germany to Norway to Scotland, and women accused of crimes such as "dancing with the devil" and casting spells on livestock were routinely and ritually burned at the stake, drowned and executed by public hanging. Their performed demise served the same purpose as Guy Fawkes' punishment — to deter others against dissent through intimidation and to strike the fear of God (and, more importantly, the state) into the hearts of the public.

Through the centuries, Western culture has both recorded and perpetuated further demonisation of villains such as these, both exposing the horror of their treatment but also, in some ways, being complicit in the perpetuation of it. Certain tropes have been used interchangeably to describe, intimidate and dehumanise whichever political group or community is out of favour — whether old Scottish pagans (usually women) resisting the misogynistic Church of Scotland or the English, or Catholics resisting the Protestant English government that was persecuting them, or Jews or Arabs merely migrating to a new city (or simply remaining in their own homes).

In recent decades, my research led me to see many centuries of persecution, othering and Orientalism coalesced in the depiction of Muslims in the War on Terror. While Islamophobia has obviously extended far beyond those actually involved in terrorist activities, in the war itself, the villains of the moment are those we call terrorists, and people who look enough like them. Terrorists, like other iconic political villains before them — whether guilty of a crime or not — fulfil an important role in our culture. They are used as scapegoats in times of social crisis, exaggerating their power and status in a form of social ritual that functions to purge communal anxiety and fear, however fleetingly.

The French anthropologist René Girard developed a theory of "the scapegoating mechanism", whereby he observed that cultures throughout history have engaged in a social ritual of demonisation and fetishisation, punishing a villain so that the community may feel absolved of its sins and related anxieties. The term "scapegoat" refers to the biblical practise of sacrificing a goat in order to atone sins of the communities, and Girard explains that the practice simply developed to replace the goat with a person, recollecting both Satan and Jesus in the containment and absolving of the sins of the people.

Stanley Cohen, an American sociologist, wrote about a similar practise that he termed "moral panics" and "folk devils". In his theory, which focussed on the idea of "deviants" demonised in a disproportionate way by communities and wider societies, he also observed that these figures become infamous, almost iconic, in representing what society deems to be evil and immoral. Connecting "moral panic" to these figures, and their necessary punishment, he also saw the crucial connection between a community's extreme panic, or anxiety, and the demonisation and destruction of the "folk devil", to use his term.

While Cohen discusses the "folk devils" of the 1970s — the "Mods and Rockers, skinheads, video nasties, designer drugs, bogus asylum seeks and hoodies" — he explains that every age has its exaggerated demons. At different points these have been single mothers, teenage mothers, hippies, refugees, Muslims, Eastern European immigrants, goths, trans people, and, further back, Catholics, pagans and so-called witches. The moral panics that are stirred up against these groups provide a mechanism whereby the wider public can focus all their energy and fear onto one simple villainous group, in a ritualistic manner that desires the symbolic destruction or purging of that group (or individual representing them), which can be galvanised for political gain. Whether as a means of distracting from other issues or demonising social groups to ensure that their grievances or problems are ignored, it is very often successful in these terms. The way in which terrorists become "folk devils" is at the extreme end of this social behaviour, and in many ways it is understandable why this should occur.

It is not at all surprising that terrorist attacks should tip communities over the edge and cause mass panic, social crisis and lasting anxiety; that is the whole point of them, after all. That the reaction to terrorist attacks is to demonise and punish either those who committed the crime or those who represent those who did, is also understandable, if also often counterproductive. What is fascinating, and disturbing, is how these events, and the reactions to them, repeat the social rituals of panic and persecution that we have seen throughout history, and often destroy those who are not guilty at all, but merely possess a superficial likeness.

The reactivity and arbitrariness of this ritualistic behaviour reveals just how emotional so many of our society's political and judicial decisions are. Entire wars are waged in knee-jerk reactions to horrific events, but in ways that do not really promise any peace or resolution. We become caught in this cycle of reactivity, whereby we cannot truly recover or progress, because we are stuck in this mentality, caught in a loop of fearfulness and rash, anxious decision-making.

It is also not surprising that this pattern of behaviour can be exploited to control the public, whether by those behind terrorist attacks or the governments reacting to them. It's not surprising that the fearfulness triggered by atrocities like terrorist attacks should be galvanised towards people who have had no part to play in causing those atrocities, and in fact may also be victims of them, because links are made by the media and our own politicians, and then ourselves or those around us, whether overtly or unconsciously.

It's natural, when something bad has happened, and the Fear does not leave us, to want or need someone to blame, and to want revenge. It is so easy to slide into projection and scapegoating without even realising it. So much of our decision-making is based on unconscious desires, not rational thoughts. "Folk devils", or "scapegoats" reflect back our fears and desires, they are created by us to deflect from our own pain and responsibility, our own fears, and move it elsewhere, in such a way that there seems an easy resolution to that terror — their destruction. We think (or feel) that if we destroy or dominate this figure, this symbol, then we will be atoned, cleansed and calmed. That things will be right again. That the pain of the wounds that have been inflicted on us will lessen.

But any such feeling is fleeting, and such reactivity does not produce lasting solutions, but instead sometimes causes lasting problems. As Girard wrote, as a society "we make martyrs of our victims". We become obsessed with blaming and sacrificing people so that we do not have to feel pain so deeply ourselves. But like any drug — any repetitive, addictive, compulsive behaviour — all we do in these cycles is defer and complicate that original pain. It does not become less unbearable over time simply through the active hatred towards another person or symbol.

On a political level, fear entwined with a desire for revenge may infer a sense of victimhood that can become toxic and misguided. If we conceptualise ourselves as the victims, first and foremost, and more so than anyone else (when this is not the case), if we think we are the most "exceptional" victims, then we assume a moral high ground that is unjustified, but seen to justify further atrocities. Such thinking is used to justify torture and drone strikes, terrorist attacks, assassinations and Islamophobia, shootings and murders. They are crimes of passion, not reason, but we rarely admit to that when they are encouraged and committed by global leaders who manipulate us to be scared and paranoid.

Applying this perspective to our own and our societies' behaviour, stretching back centuries, it becomes clear that these knee-jerk, passionate, often sanctimonious reactions to fear are commonly weaponised for political gain, and often in such a way that the most vulnerable in society suffer the most for crimes they did not commit. At the root of this reactive behaviour is powerlessness, or at least the perception of it. Those who are insecure and perceive themselves to be lacking power and control choose a symbolic villain through which to vicariously play out the grievances they have experienced. They project onto this figure their crises and traumas — sometimes because that figure has indeed done something horrific, but sometimes just because they symbolise "evil" in a superficial, socially constructed manner that is not personal or particular at all. Scapegoating can be quite arbitrary in this sense.

The interesting thing about terrorism, to me, was that as a political phenomenon, it had grown out of a morality system that elevates martyrdom and the moral high ground of the aggrieved. The men who flew planes into the Twin Towers, killing thousands, thought of themselves as martyrs. They then inspired those moved by the horrors of that day to sacrifice themselves in battle, too, or to sacrifice other people. When people claim the role of "terrorist", they do so as they claim the role of martyr. They think what they are doing is good and honourable. Both sides are aggrieved, and both claim legitimacy either morally or legally for the hurt they then cause. These are martyrs who want to be feared as well as glorified; these sacrificial actions are intended, ultimately, to gain power. Both sides will say the same things — that they sacrifice themselves to save others — and as they do so, they are playing out similar roles. Both will be demonised by the other side, too.

As I studied further, I became fascinated about how fear interrelated with morality, along with power and powerlessness, sacrifice and scapegoating, and how all of these things together caused conflict that persisted, stuck in a loop of reactivity. Resentment from pain — whether actual or imagined, direct or at a distance — was forever used to justify performed violence and fear-mongering in drawn out, tit-for-tat conflicts that draw on religious rituals and ideas of "goodness" as inextricably linked to sacrifice.

The state of fear, then, is invoked and provoked in such a way as to galvanise trauma to justify even more violence. In this way, such fear constitutes and defines reality, taking individual emotional reactions to trauma, and connected feelings of powerlessness, to transform the political landscape and then take decisions based on those heavily manipulated perceptions of threat and what such threats should justify in the way of retaliation.

—

As the months went on, I collected hundreds of pictures of these terrorists, the villains and victims before them, and tabloid front pages, strewn across my desk and room. I put them into carefully organised books, and highlighted the main themes, stories and features. After all of this, and after seeing the Abu Ghraib pictures hundreds of times, as well as lynching photographs and other horrible images, I first became depressed by the violence, then sort of desensitised and then almost phobic of them. I had looked at them so many times, trying to do so in a detached way, out of necessity, because I was studying them — until I couldn't look at them at all, and even a glance at one would make me recoil.

I had thought so much about the stories told through these images and the power plays that they performed, but the violence of them or what they represented never went away. All that I could control was how much I looked at them. But even then, I was writing about them, and no matter how much work I did, how I deconstructed the symbols and meaning, the way they connected to one another, how they were framed in history or the press — I still looked at them afresh and felt only a numb sort of horror. These were people. They had been people. Now there were just these photographs.

Conceptually, I drew a blank. None of it was real; that was the point. The people had been real, but these photographs were not them, did not explain anything more. They did not answer whatever it was I was looking for. I ended up back where I had begun: who was behind the mask, behind the story, behind the photos? Who were these people, and how did they feel, and why did these images and stories feel so detached from their realities? Why did we all live in this strange, mediated way, living life through the spectacle, as Guy Debord had foreseen, existing at one remove, as Plato had, too? Why was I doing this and what was the point, when knowing more would not stop the reality of what had already happened, would not really explain why people blew up thousands of people, or waged wars on the wrong targets, or created mayhem?

Behind all of this research, for me, was the same existential crisis, the same void, which was also at the heart of war. None of it made sense. The desire for affirmation is not the same as having it; if anything, it betrays a lack of it. Telling stories of the deceased will not bring them back; understanding what made someone infamous doesn't really make sense of their crimes. Telling stories of villains will not rid the world of them, however awful and monstrous we portray them to be. I was deconstructing the stories people tell each other, which set the scene for war, as if that could help me understand why war existed. And it did; I understood how one thing led to another, how fear made people killers as often as victims. But understanding it didn't negate the horror I still felt. I realised that the Fear, this common existential crisis, was not simply about fearing one's own mortality, but also about fearing the presence of other people, as if the presence of another might threaten one's own reality.

In war, and in peace, we struggle to co-exist and to connect. We struggle to reconcile our own human existence with that of others. How can we share a world with people who would kill and maim and rape others? How can we ever understand what another person is suffering? How can we live when another is dying? Something gnawed at me then, and since; how could I be content in this reality, being aware of what I was aware of? How could I be happy any other way than escaping consciousness itself?

I'm not sure whether it was survivors' guilt or basic compassion, or my own neurosis or self-sabotage, but whenever I thought of my father or the wars I was studying, or when I watched the news — which was much of the time — it seemed almost unethical, and impossible, to be happy. It also felt futile to be unhappy and anxious when I had a life to live, when I was not in a war, when my father was still alive, when there was so much to be thankful for. I began to realise that I had caught myself in a trap: I was overanalysing myself, and my own feelings, and those of other people. I was telling myself stories, in a way — to rationalise emotions I could never hope to fully rationalise. I could not think myself out of feeling. I could not escape my basic instincts, even if the basic instinct was to worry, and to write, and to freeze in this perpetual angst. I was using thinking itself as a form of escapism. It wasn't working. I was escaping myself to the point of disassociation.

There were no answers here; or rather, answers were not what I really wanted. I wanted to understand and know people, and I was also scared of them. I wanted love, I wanted peace. This was not where I could find it.

I had wanted my father, but he wasn't really there. At times, he seemed no more real or present than these pictures in the papers, of feared, distant, complex men either dead or imprisoned now, or searched for by the world's armies.

I wanted to know them, or know more about them, or at least know how their existence slotted into the rest of human life. I wanted to reconcile myself with their existence, and the existence of other men I had feared in my life — to find some peace, to get along better with the devil on my shoulder, to diffuse the phantoms, analyse them to dust.

And yet, as Nietzsche had warned, the abyss stared back, and it captured me, and for quite some time I forgot myself entirely, distracted by this project, this obsession I had committed myself to, in denial about its function in my own life as a distraction from feeling my own pain, as well as spiritual doubt and disillusionment. I was writing about fear but the writing itself was a way to avoid fully feeling it, fully submitting to its emotional and spiritual power over me.

Notes from an Abyss

At some point, having read a lot of criminology, psychology and anthropology — about radicalisation, the nature of evil and trauma — I found myself at a loss, and picked up an old copy of Nietzsche's *Beyond Good and Evil*.[6] This wasn't directly related to my thesis, and I didn't especially want to write about Nietzsche, and yet I ended up back there out of some desire for comfort as much as anything. That may seem strange, for Nietzsche is hardly "comforting", but it brought me back to a place, perhaps the beginning of this philosophical journey, when I had first picked up *Thus Spoke Zarathustra* at school, aged fifteen.

It hadn't really made any sense to me then, and yet there was some emotional force to Nietzsche's elaborate and pained writings which somehow consoled me. He is the angstiest of the philosophers, I suppose, and though I did not find any consoling meaning in anything he wrote, that was itself consoling. His writing seemed to be a sort of ballad, as much as a theoretical text; whatever the content of his work, his frustration, desire and pain was so barely concealed, regardless of his sophisticated reason and argument, that I felt strangely content when I read his work. What that "meant", I didn't know, then. I just knew that I ended up reading Nietzsche

---

6   Friedrich Nietzsche, *Beyond Good and Evil.* Penguin Classics; Reissue edition, 2003.

again, all these years later, when I could not look at pictures of terrorists any longer.

And though I had not really gone to him for answers — rather for a sort of angsty camaraderie — it turned out that Nietzsche did have some useful ideas after all! All these pictures of villains, all this darkness and pain, all these emotional rituals of scapegoating and victimhood, and of course Nietzsche had been there all along. I could not understand fear, or guilt, or shame, without understanding its relation to power. I couldn't understand how evil happened without understanding, first, what it meant to perform victimhood and self-righteousness. I couldn't understand conflict without realising the animalistic, desperate and yet cunning ruthlessness of humans. I couldn't resurrect my desire for life itself, really, without embracing the true nihilism so present in human nature, too.

—

In *The Genealogy of Morals* and *Beyond Good and Evil*, Nietzsche presents the idea of *"ressentiment"*, in which, as a result of pain rooted in one's own sense of powerlessness or inferiority, we project or reassign that pain to an external scapegoat. We blame another person or symbol and cast them as an enemy and as "evil" in order to blame them for the hurt and fear we experience, rather than take responsibility for it ourselves. *Ressentiment* is related to Sigmund Freud's ideas about ego and projection, as well as René Girard's concept of the scapegoating mechanism, and indeed, these theorists are indebted to Nietzsche on those points.

According to Nietzsche, *ressentiment* is rooted in what he terms "the slave mentality". Weakness confers reactiveness; if someone is weak then they will be overly reactive, whereas if one is active and strong, a "master", then they will not overthink their problems and grievances, considering themselves to be a victim of life and others, but rather they will embrace life and their own possibility and passion. For "slaves" however, their *ressentiment* is galvanised into a moral system — what Nietzsche terms "slave morality", which makes a virtue out of weakness, sacrifice and martyrdom, and conversely defines the "masters" as bad due to their choices to be rich and powerful at the expense of others.

Victimhood is central to this morality system; the endurance of suffering is a source of virtue and personal value. While Nietzsche understood that this gave the weak and powerless a new, transformative moral power that they did not possess before, he criticised this approach to morality as inherently nihilistic, as it made a virtue out of lack and resentment. It empowered the powerless but this power was delusional, in that it was not material or physical power, but a construction, a new, invented moral code that did not embrace or change life, did not tolerate other moral ideas or allow either the slaves or the masters true freedom, as he saw it.

Crucially, the slave morality — by which he meant Judeo-Christian religion — was based on fear as much as resentment; "hell" was invented to deter through intimidation and terror, to control through emotional manipulation, coercion and a "mob mentality". Nietzsche considered this mindset and approach to life as "life-denying". It was to live in fear and to inflict that fear on others, rather than embracing life. To act against this descent into nihilism, Nietzsche wanted to evolve past the slave-master dichotomy, writing about possible ways in which people might live and progress by taking elements of both slave and master mentalities, and aimed to move beyond both. Writing about figures he called at times "the Free

Spirit", the "*Übermensch*" and "the Sovereign Individual",[7] he suggested that we might escape the bind of the slave morality, but also move beyond the limitations of the master mentality by forging a new path and leaving this social dynamic in favour of true freedom, both material and mental. In fact, he saw Jesus Christ as a form of *Übermensch*, possessing both the "nobility" of the masters and the better qualities of the "slave mentality" to be truly transgressive, transformational and progressive.[8]

Nietzsche's idea was a development from both the master and slave positions, in which one consciously emerges from this dynamic — and especially the "slave mentality" part of it — to become a free individual. In this idealistic state, one is not dependent on anyone else or at the mercy of an authority or God, not deemed to sacrifice oneself perpetually, but instead free to live and find meaning in the world on one's own terms. Crucially, one lives fearlessly, or at least boldly — not dwelling on threat or angst, but moving forward with strength and bravery. Rather than turning inward and fearing God and the power of other people, Nietzsche's free spirit turns outwards, planted in the real world and embracing freedom wherever possible, rather than the bonds of human and societal relations, which would leave one fearful and reactive.

Such an ideal is not attractive to everyone, of course, or even remotely possible. Many people simply cannot escape the human relationships and societal bonds that Nietzsche would have us discard (and regardless of their difficulty, would not want to). I often wonder, too, if Nietzsche overlooked the

---

7   Friedrich Nietzsche, *Beyond Good and Evil.* Penguin Classics; Reissue
     edition, 2003.

8   Ibid.

complex, even noble reasons that people may wish to remain enslaved by either morality or human relationships, beyond resentment, weakness or lack of imagination.

Hegel gave some insight into the complexity of the "slave master relationship" in *The Phenomenology of Spirit* when he suggested that the slave (which could symbolise either a part of oneself or of society), could find meaning and growth — transcendence — within their powerless position, as they would eventually find inner strength through submission, self-reflection and work, and so transcend their physical status.[9] The master, however, would always be stuck in this dynamic, always dependent on the slave to feel power, strength and affirmation, but never finding it within, and never transcending the dynamic. Ultimately, however, "slavery belongs to a necessary stage of history before the formation of states. It has to be replaced by legal relations between equal 'persons.'"[10]

How does this relate to fear and the state of fearfulness that is part of the human condition? In my own experience, especially during that time after I graduated, it was impossible to be free when crushed by a chronic sense of anxiety and insecurity; regardless of the immediacy of the object of fear, to live in this heightened, paralysed way was oppressive in itself. As I understood it, Nietzsche's work suggested that this state of mind, this neurosis, was entangled with a morality system that was based on resentment, fear and shame, and to be free of that state, one would therefore need to escape the

---

9   G. W. F. Hegel, *The Phenomenology of Spirit.* Oxford University Press, U.S.A.; Revised ed. edition, 30 Nov. 1976.

10   Ludwig Siep, "Hegel on the Master Slave Relation", *Fifteen Eight Four: Academic Perspectives from Cambridge University Press,* 02 May 2014.

shackles of that entire worldview and the social structures that went with it. Hegel, meanwhile, seemed to imply that it could be possible to develop oneself despite those structures and powerlessness — that through work and self-development, for instance, one could transcend oppression mentally, even if not in a physical sense.

Both the Nietzschean and Hegelian interpretations intrigued me when I had first come across them as an undergraduate, and now again as I studied terrorism and how people reacted to it. I was interested in the idea that it was possible to find serenity and transcendence through submission and work, but also by the idea of true "radical" freedom and self-determination. In a way, both ideas aimed for the same result — a sense of individual freedom, regardless of whether that meant true physical liberation or not (and whatever sacrifice that implied).

The Fear was itself a sort of paralysis which was caused by powerlessness; it was the clear emotional consequence of that state. The threats I perceived in everyday life may have seemed diffuse, but they were nevertheless real, and they were all rooted in a lack of power. Why was I scared? Because I had little control over how men treated me, in the past and even in the present. I felt powerlessness, or I remembered being truly powerless, and this state of weakness continued to haunt me.

I felt powerless in my own life, and in the lives of others; I could not know when my father would die, or when my next pay cheque was coming in (or how much of the tiny PhD stipend would be left after bills), or where I was living in the next month. I could not know who was trustworthy and who wasn't. This sense of powerlessness was at the root of the Fear.

I had learnt to project my panic onto whatever was in my midst in the present moment that was remotely threatening

— a man walking behind me at night, an unreliable date, a random person's bad mood. I had many real reasons to be afraid and traumatised, but I could not face those, so I became a fearful person who saw threat everywhere, despite every effort to be free and bold. The Fear was not something I could just switch off or leave behind. However, by seeking to understand it better, I began to deconstruct it in myself, too.

I became ever more fascinated in how fear was used to acquire political power, and how people were so often encouraged to be afraid of some people and threats more than others, depending on the political landscape, when underlying their sense of fear was really their own lack of power, and sometimes the trauma of powerlessness over years and generations. Scapegoating stood out as a social practise that ritualised this desire to blame someone else for one's own sense of powerlessness and trauma, and the resentment that it caused, in a way that was especially relevant to how society dealt with political violence.

I was interested in how society more generally thought about those who are termed "terrorists". They were depicted as devils, villains, the ultimate threat and fear in our modern age. There were people who had done terrible things, clearly, but these individuals were somewhat distinct from the puppet-like villains who were splashed across the tabloids and set on fire as effigies. Terrorists were modern scapegoats in the sense that they were symbols of evil whose ritualistic demise would help people feel better and more united in the wake of social crisis.

As I collected and analysed yet more images of Bin Laden and Saddam Hussein, the Boston Bombers and others, putting together the early stages of a theory about rituals of fetishisation and communal purging, it also occurred to me I had replaced my own confusions in my personal life with this new academic project. I had replaced trying to understand those who had hurt me, with learning about these infamous figures who had been deemed evil by the society I had grown up in and which had formed me. My patterns of behaviour, in my personal life, and the ways in which I dealt with trauma and crisis, could be identified in much wider terms in the world around me. The fetishisation of these feared male villains, these bad guys, these violent, abusive monsters, was a ritual deeply embedded in this Western culture, and also in my own heart.

As a society we were obsessed, however unconsciously, with those who hurt and terrified us; we were entranced by and stuck in rituals of their downfall and our own. In moments of crisis, we respond, as individuals and communities, in many fascinating and often disturbing ways. In my own life, I had projected my abandonment and abuse issues onto other men, or found other men who would go on to repeat my greatest fears, and as a society we also exaggerated the threat and power of certain villains so as to contain our communal fears — but also to distract from them. In so doing, we only provoked more violence, more terror, in a repetitive tit-for-tat war of optics and drone warfare. We focussed more on punishing the villains and not on ourselves, distracting from the pain but not healing from it, and not transcending it. We were neither masters nor free spirits; we were slaves, and not especially enlightened ones.

—

The pressure to be threatening is part of masculinity, and to be intimidating and feared is a masculine virtue. The projection of fear — onto women, or those who show their masculinity in alternate ways — is generally rooted in insecurity, the fear that one is not man enough, or that the performance of masculinity may be seen through, that the mask may slip and reveal someone who is as vulnerable as anyone else. The weakness of men is well known and well observed, and yet it comes with so much baggage and drama, so much guilt and shame. Such weakness is therefore repressed, or at least hidden from view. Vulnerability is concealed, as if to fail at masculinity, to lapse into femininity, would be the worst thing in the world.

But that vulnerability remains, regardless, and when it is felt, the only socially acceptable reaction, for a man invested in the patriarchy, is to be angry rather than sad, violent rather than upset. Emotional reactions (to fear, say) tend to be channelled into "masculine" expressions rather than more "feminine" and peaceful or nurturing alternatives, because men are expected to be emotional only in a masculine manner, rather than feminine. As such, it is hardly surprising that whether in personal settings, political life or global conflicts, the emotional reactions to tensions, based in fear or related trauma or victimhood, are typically "masculine" in their energy and expression. We are so used to all of this, and masculine emotional expression is so normal, that it is hard to imagine a world in which other emotional expressions may take precedence. Masculinity, and the masculine expressions of fear, define political violence and how conflict is played out in a general sense. It also defines how morality is invoked to justify such conflict.

Perpetrators of terror, for instance, who use performed violence to intimidate and crush their enemies, typically make an effort to justify their actions, in line with patriarchal ideologies. They are righteous and brave, they imply, simply getting justice and protecting those who cannot fight for themselves. They are only to be feared by those who are already damned or inferior to them; they are basically good people.

Although in certain cases — like Abu Ghraib — those involved in the abuse will be condemned and even apologise themselves, usually acts of terror and torture are only condemned by those outside the perpetrators' own communities. In effect, any ideas of goodness are defined by the group or community and they can be bended to accommodate any atrocities required. In patriarchal societies, it follows that ideas of goodness are usually wound up with (and defined by) ideas about gender.

Masculinity forgives a lot (to men anyway); as long as a man is seen to be acting with strength and power, and somehow protecting women and children (however vaguely), his actions are usually seen as defensible. Being threatening is part of being masculine; patriarchy as an ideology justifies and relies on terror and everyday fearfulness to persist. Fear is its fuel and its characteristic.

As such, being terroristic — so long as it is very blatantly masculine, and accompanied by rhetoric to that effect — is often also seen as being sort of good, at least to the perpetrator's own community. It is a masculine virtue, an expression of masculinity in its purest form. Many people therefore embrace this idea of being "bad" and threatening because it is also "good" — so long as it is man enough and targeted at the right enemies.

I think of abusers as I write this, shackled to misogynistic ideas of what men should be allowed to do and the limits of their available emotional outlets and expressions. I also think about terrorists and prime ministers and politicians, of course, and the masculine role they are expected to fulfil (regardless of sex). I think about how so many men will, when pressed, revert back, whether they're aware of it or not, to patriarchy as the ideology that justifies their behaviour. "I'm a man and I'm angry!" they might insist (or words to that effect). Or "I'm doing this for you!" Or perhaps more insidious, subtle approaches — if one's (male) friends or political colleagues are also lying and cheating and getting into fights, then it seems normal and therefore permissible. Being angry and avoidant and reckless isn't a personal failure, it isn't just selfish; it's being a man. Masculinity entails this violence and egotism. It is utterly normalised and endemic.

Sometimes, however, perpetrators of terror, whether state-led or sub-state, embrace the idea of being "bad" more overtly or shamelessly as a form of justified retribution. Much of this is still related to ideas of masculinity, consciously or unconsciously. What could be more masculine than violence or even full-blown war, after all? The idea of the "strong" formidable, ruthless man also recalls Nietzsche's "masters", who were supposed to be mostly unthinking "warriors" who did not dwell on pain but fought it out.

Quite often, though, when a political actor is performing violence in this way, they are very evidently embracing a sense of their own victimhood — Nietzsche's "slave mentality" — as a way to justify their actions. They are only embracing their ruthless, evil actions as "retribution" because someone else started it first, after all. And they are doing so, crucially, as a way of undermining the masculinity of their enemies. To be most masculine, there is a pressure to be most violent, to reclaim and refashion the "barbarism" that has been levelled at them and elevate it to a higher form of masculinity.

In this sense, the very structure of our societies is rooted in this patriarchal *"ressentiment"*, this routine projection of domestic insecurities onto "other" enemies, seeming to justify terror, and the social rituals of scapegoating and demonisation explored by Girard and Cohen. We cannot blame only others for what is surely a communal disease, bred in everyday life, not merely on the battlefield. Everyone is implicated in the cultural justification of this terroristic behaviour.

But why was the bad guy both attractive and formidable to so many, and what do these men represent to those who follow or desire them? How can this toxic masculinity (and not all masculinity must necessarily be so toxic) be disrupted and resisted? How could we ever move on from *ressentiment* to true freedom? To understand how to break free, I realised that I first needed to ask what it was about this cage, these prison guards and this painful game that was still found by so many (and perhaps even myself, on some level) to be appealing, or at least excusable, often despite our best intentions or best interests, and those of others. Why did we accept the arbitrary discipline and amorality of those who asserted that they had authority, simply because they were so intimidating?

I realised that it was important to understand that there was pleasure in the performance and embodiment of masculinity, and in the masculine expressions of and reactions to fear. Within certain social settings and having been brought up to appreciate and enjoy the ego boost that comes from being seen as masculine, there are clear incentives to act in this way and to accept this behaviour in others. People want to be feared, whether intentionally or subconsciously, and they also want to be feared, and therefore secure, by association. They are competitive about who is perceived to be stronger and more powerful, and making other people scared is how this dominance is asserted.

Power is a drug, and if it can be fleetingly experienced through the destruction of other people and the vicarious dominance of allies, then this is often a price worth paying, for some people. Especially if one's own emotional expression is repressed and controlled, it is easy to see why the relief from masculine emotional reactions — through violence or other means — is compelling and addictive to so many. On the flip side, there are reasons why people accept and even glorify these masculine emotional reactions and this image of powerfulness, even as it damages them. There are reasons people allow the power-grabs of others, even when it doesn't benefit them — and it is not always as simple as fearing the powerful.

Love is complicated. While it may not seem at first glance to be relevant to a discussion of fear, especially related to global politics, I think that it is crucial. Out of love, one will surrender power, because submission is the denial of oneself, and assuages fear and insecurity by giving the responsibility for oneself to another. In politics and personal life, it is normal to defer, to submit, to bow down — not simply out of fear for that person, but out of love for them, and the faith that in giving up one's power, one will be ultimately stronger, because one is then a part of that other, more powerful force.

Collective power relies on this deference of individual power, and it is explained by faith, by patriotism — by forms of love, basically — and at root, the desire to be part of something more powerful than one could ever be alone. When this love becomes toxic (and it is not necessarily so), when it is entangled with submission and masochism and romanticism, it can be used to justify and enable the tyranny of toxic masculinity, because it allows and desires unchecked power for the sake of vicarious pleasure, and the relief of being saved from fear at the expense of others and even oneself.

Humans want to worship something bigger than themselves, and if they don't fear God, they will find someone else to deify and submit to, so as to escape or absolve the inherent insecurity and precarity of life itself. This can be a sort of love — a romantic love, a toxic love. To be the couple in the corner of the Breughel painting, escaping death and oblivious to war. This is a sort of love, the best-known kind, at least. For a long time, it was the only kind I knew.

This love was primarily an escape, each relationship a way to turn away from the darkness of the world, fleetingly at least, until it found its way in anyway. There was always something fatalistic to my approach to love; I lived as if I would die any second, or they would, or we all would. I had grown up always on the verge of bereavement, and so intrinsically worried — but also assumed — that any love would be gone soon. My love was defensive and nervous, and looking back, I locked myself into relationships in such a way that I tricked myself. I could not be myself in them; I had suppressed my own sense of freedom and expansiveness, of adventure. I was a slave to love, and I could not really imagine a love in which I was truly free. I accepted this strange isolation, this wanting, this worrying, this fearful love.

But inevitably the Fear remained and returned; despite any new happiness I found, a part of me remained heartbroken and anxious, as if waiting for imminent loss. This became a self-fulfilling prophecy. Subconsciously, I chose precariousness and distance, I chose risk and difficulty. I had a masochistic streak, not simply in relation to people but in how I spent all of my time. I was writing a thesis on terrorists, I was trying to understand the unfathomable; I was trying to make peace with the devil. I was attempting the impossible, and then reprimanding myself when there were no answers or real consolations, when things inevitably fell apart.

My entire PhD was a coping mechanism, and yet I couldn't see that at all; I simply grew more and more frustrated that all the analysis in the world could not make me *feel* any differently, could not close a wound, could not really even protect against a threat. And yet, I kept at it, in vain, addicted to the pain I could not quite articulate, which attracted me, on some level, as it repelled and traumatised me, too.

A Masochistic Education

After the Boston Bombings, *Rolling Stone* magazine published an issue in which a hazy portrait of one of the perpetrators made the cover. There was outrage that a terrorist, someone who had very recently killed and maimed many innocent people, was treated very literally like a rock star. It was jarring, and people were hurt. But it's worth exploring further why *Rolling Stone* equated a young terrorist to a rock star, where these performances overlap, and what this says about a wider, conflicted relationship with "the bad boy" in Western culture especially.

We should be afraid of them, or at least turned off by them, and yet we are often (also) attracted to them. It is a joke and an indulgence at times, but also a reality: our culture and many individuals love the idea of the rogue, the bad boy. Fear doesn't deter attraction at all; sometimes, instead, it inflames it. We want what is bad for us, it would appear — in a fervoured, masochistic, romantic obsession. And our culture can't get enough of these stories, whether or not anyone officially approves of those involved. From the portrayal of Jihadi brides willing to die for their men by ISIS propagandists, to Lana Del Rey's ballads of doomed love and toxic rogues, why are people so compelled by masochistic, self-sabotaging desire, or at least stories of it? Why do we desire what is so bad for us, and why does a haze of nostalgia follow individuals who are so destructive? What makes people masochistic? Why do we lean into our own gilded oppression?

If sadists and Machiavellians embrace the fears of others so fervently, then masochists seem, at first glance, to embrace their own fears in a self-destructive and yet cathartic compulsion to surrender. When faced with danger, we typically experience a "fight or flight" response, with "flight" manifesting as many different behaviours, from disassociating, fawning or people-pleasing, becoming avoidant, or simply running away. With this in mind, it's possible to see how surrendering to an abuser, or simply a person one fears, may be a typical if destructive response to both immediate threat and the cyclical effects of living with unresolved past trauma.

In my own life, I had always been attracted to the bad boys, often apparently unaware that they could be genuinely dangerous or abusive (rather than just exciting or charming) until many months into a relationship, seemingly unable to see the red flags others may have seen clearly. Even when I was aware of the red flags, I wanted to stay, because I loved them, and could not imagine life without them. I would know that everything was wrong and demeaned — I knew about all the lies and manipulation and undermining, the lack of care — and yet I did not want to let go, and so for as long as I could, I did not let go. I always held out that perhaps they could change, get better, and perhaps I could help them.

My weakness felt like a strength — it felt like love, like the closest, realest thing. The idea of willingly saying goodbye to that — and to the one I so deeply adored — felt like sacrilege. I was absolutely a slave to love, a hopeless romantic. I could not understand love without sacrifice, because it was all I had ever known. Even when I lost myself in these situations, I wanted to stay, to not be left. The losing myself part was, perhaps, I see now, a part of the attraction, if it meant that the person I loved stayed, if we could be together, transformed (for better or worse) into something more than our broken selves. I feared abandonment, and I feared myself. I feared change, feared letting go. Chaos in a person I loved, and in a relationship with them, seemed preferable to the chaos and emptiness — the fearfulness — of being alone.

Over the years, and several relationships alike in this way, I realised that masochism is more complex than being simply a trauma response, or merely a form of "flight" or "freeze" when faced with danger. It was something I really chased, however unconsciously. It was something that, on some level, I wanted to experience again and again and again, as if I would somehow know more or feel more if I kept chasing what I could not have and was not supposed to want. It was an act of rebellion, a search for impossible freedom. My life felt empty without the extremes of emotion, the turbulence of toxic love. I missed it whenever it was gone. I was addicted to it, in a way, and this desire would eclipse my own sense of self-preservation and sense.

In some attempt to understand and override whatever was compelling me to be this way, I first looked to Sigmund Freud, who explored masochism as a challenge to what he termed "the Pleasure Principle", essentially the will to self-preservation and life itself. Why did people do things, often many times over and compulsively, which were obviously bad for them? Why did some people seem to chase pain and their own destruction? He developed a theory of what is known as the "death drive", the idea that even though we, as humans, have a will to live, we also have a will to die, to retreat from life, and crucially to have some control over that eventuality (however contrived). "The organism seeks to die in its own way", he wrote, and as death is inevitable and a part of life itself, people are also affected by the desire to define their own ends, their own destruction — or at least to entertain the fantasy that they can control the contours of their own life.

Freud also wrote about the "Compulsion to Repeat" which he saw as a drive distinct from the Pleasure Principle. Here, by repeating experiences, people transform their relationship to those original experiences and often diminish the power that the root memory, or fear, has on them. In a sense, by reclaiming a traumatic memory, for example, by repeating it on one's own terms, one may diminish its power and hold.

In particular, Freud wrote about "the repeated departure" in relationship to masochistic pleasure, which is "less evident because it is the opposite of *good sense*, which assumes the sad and painful form of a repeated departure". He discusses a childhood game, in which the child expresses, and so learns about, the tragic nature of human experience, about the loss inherent to life itself. "Finding the object is never other than finding it once more. The encounter with the object (of love) masks and erases what truly constitutes the object in itself: its loss. The object is lost, not by misfortune or chance, but by its essence."[11]

> Love is held by a thread, something at the very heart of the drive opposes its full satisfaction, the experience of the loss constitutes the object... and so be it! We cure evil with evil, poke a painful tooth with the tip of our tongue, derive pleasure from the loss if that is what love means [*cultivons à plaisir la perte si c'est ce qu'amour veut dire*]. In this primary, immanent or radical form, masochism is wed to the generic form

---

11   Sigmund Freud, "Beyond the Pleasure Principle", *SE*, 18, pp. 7-60.

of melancholy. Sexuality takes its revenge and invests, at the very heart of that which gives it birth, its own limit. The impossibility of satisfaction, the deferred fulfilment of desire, in short, disappointed love, cease to contravene the desired aim to become the aim itself.[12]

This melancholic nature that expresses itself in repeated departures, in a sort of indulgence in the tragedy of love and loss, and indeed life itself, can begin to explain why we, as humans, become involved in compulsive patterns of pain and self-denial in reaction to fear.

It also gives insight into the role of fantasy and contrived, masochistic situations or cycles in which pleasure is derived from the control one has over a scenario, rather than just the scenario itself; the masochist, after all, is typically, on some level, in control of the painful situation they seem to submit themselves to. They are the architects of their own pain and humiliation, and so that pain may feel like a form of empowerment, however counter-intuitive. They do not have to fear what they are in some way in control of or emotionally detached from. As Jacques André has written of this phenomenon:

> The perversion repeats the "actual" bodily attack, it conserves the tight and monotonous rhythm of the traumatic neurosis, yet the fact that the pain is staged and sexualized marks the distance the subject has taken.[13]

---

12 Jacques André, "Immanent Masochism", in the *European Journal of Psychoanalysis* (1920)

13 Ibid.

We repeat painful things that have been done to us with the crucial difference that, in the new situation, we have some level of distance or control which we did not have before.

Although many of Freud's theories have been challenged in the century since they were published, this idea about masochistic behaviours following childhood trauma (in particular) resonates with more recent research into PTSD, and how the mind becomes stuck in a loop, in a sense, in a dysregulated "fight or flight" mode, where responses become defined by a past trauma. In this sense, the traumatised individual is prone to cyclical behaviour in which any lasting release or peace from anxiety and anguish is hard to access. Therein, addictive or compulsive behaviours, in which the individual repeats a contrived version of the original trauma, becomes a default behaviour very hard to escape from.

Modern psychologists such as Gabor Maté and Besser van der Kolk talk of the need to "rewire" the brain using various strategies, after it and the entire nervous system have become dysregulated and "short-circuited" due to trauma and stress.[14] Masochistic tendencies, in this sense, can be understood as the learned behaviours or habits of a traumatised individual seeking relief and incremental power over their own unresolved pasts. The problem, of course, is that by repeating painful scenarios, even if they provide temporary relief through a power shift, can also in themselves complicate and even deepen the original trauma.

Moreover, one need not necessarily have experienced a particular trauma to act in this way; if Freud was correct in

---

14   See: Gabor Maté, *When the Body Says No: The Cost of Hidden Stress,* Vermillion, 2019, and Besser van der Kolk, *The Body Keeps The Score: Brain, Mind and Body in the Healing of Trauma,* Penguin Books, 2015.

picking up on the inherent tragedy of life — that we lose it, ultimately, and we lose those we need and love — then we can understand trauma in a far wider sense, for the purpose of understanding seemingly masochistic practices. Masochism, in this way, is a logical response to human existence, which is tragic and fleeting. By embracing the suffering in a ritualistic and symbolic way, we confront and meditate on this melancholic truth, we accept our fates and selves for what they are — precarious and vulnerable.

Jacques Lacan developed his own theory of *jouissance* in response to Freud's ideas, which provide further insight into the phenomenon of masochism, insofar as desire itself is compulsive and somewhat detached from the satisfaction of one's needs.[15] As Nietzsche also said, "It is the desire, not the desired, that we love".[16] Lacan, following Freud, understood that desire, whether sexual or otherwise, is more complex that fulfilling one's basic needs or finding straightforward pleasure; we do not always want what we need, and vice versa. There is pleasure to be found in the striving itself, in the tension of the chase and the ambivalence and even fear it may cause. As he wrote, "the subject does not simply satisfy desire, he enjoys desiring (*jouit de désirer*) and this is an essential dimension of his *jouissance*".[17] We want what we cannot have, what we are not allowed, what is not good or right. We want bad and harmful things: why?

---

15   See Darian Leader, *Jouissance: Sexuality, Suffering and Satisfaction,* Polity, 2021.

16   Friedrich Nietzsche, *Beyond Good and Evil.* Penguin Classics; Reissue edition, 2003.

17   Yorgos Dimitriadis, "The Psychoanalytic Concept of Jouissance and the Kindling Hypothesis", in *Frontiers in Psychology*, 21 September 2017.

Evidently there is an eroticism interconnected with a surrender and even chasing of ambivalence, chaos and precarity — of loss itself. There is also something compelling about indulging in the behaviour of the *femme fatale*, for instance — to be the siren, the death wish, the doomed romantic, the fallen woman. It's an act of rebellion. There is something tempting and satisfying about giving in to these things and therefore surrendering to chaos, in another person and oneself. There is something about admitting one's fallibility, one's weakness, one's worthlessness, even, and perhaps a peace to be found.

We can still understand this behaviour as a form of "fight or flight", a perpetuation of unresolved trauma through cycles of pain and relief, which can be addictive and compulsive. Trauma is not unusual; in fact, trauma is usually a part of life. We are primed to live with and react to it, and such a life may inevitably involve suffering. This fact perhaps helps to explain why people are set up to lean into their own suffering to some degree, in some effort to reconcile with it and learn to live with it. Freud intuited this existential state when he wrote about the "death drive", which was an articulation of behaviours he had observed in his own clients.

It seems clear, now as then, that we do not always want what is good for us or other people. We indulge in our dark sides, our shadows, because they offer us some feeling of connection, of truth even, about ourselves and our experiences, and our capacities to relate to others in whatever way feels right. They allow us to repeat what we don't understand, what we have loved and lost, what we need but can't have, what has hurt us, confused us and trapped us. We make peace with our own ends before death itself has come. We meet it halfway. We tease it with self-destructive behaviours, with submission on our own terms, and therein lies both the beauty and madness of being alive and wanting.

So we fawn and kneel before our oppressors; we defer to those who may destroy us, we tell them we are worthless, that we deserve what is coming to us, that we expected this all along. If we do so, after all, then how can we be disappointed, when these states, and our own weakness, are confirmed? Masochism, sometimes, is a kind of avoidance strategy. If I say I am not worth more, if I defer to the person I am afraid of, who is a genuine threat, then I do not let myself hope that I might deserve better than this. On some level, I do not believe it is possible.

The assertion that I am powerless has been internalised. My imagination, any utopian thinking, has been dulled down and forgotten. I deny my own reality, and the potential of a better one, to soften the blow, to take the edge off the betrayal of one person over another, and the disillusionment so central to that. This is a trauma response, but it is also an existential crisis; the two, I think, are inevitably entangled. I was scared of the void, or the fearful, anxious emptiness not only of being alone, but of being misunderstood. The bad boys, for all their flaws, somehow connected in this way, or gave the impression they did. They were also scared; the same emotional state inspired both abuse and the tolerance of it.

Masochism is a response to powerlessness and the invasive fearfulness that it causes, and it can certainly make life more bearable, in some cases. It can be comforting to think that someone else is so valuable and important that this trumps their toxic behaviour towards us. But we can never be free, or truly powerful or secure in ourselves, when we take this approach.

Masochism is part of the social and political conditioning we are subject to, however, and it can be hard to realise, because it is so subconscious. It is also heavily gendered and romantic, present in so many cultural narratives of love and sacrifice that are difficult to remove ourselves from entirely. It can seem impossible to detach from the narratives and political ideologies we take for granted, and instead to see other people as more complex than the roles they are assigned in life.

—

In politics and culture alike, the idea of masochism ties into romantic, heavily gendered narratives of "fallen women", which have real-life consequences for women everywhere. While the idea of the "bad boy" is at first glance comical and even arousing — not to mention the real-life manifestations — the romantic disasters we are all familiar with — the emotional manipulation and power struggles that "the bad boy" symbolises — are crucial to better understanding why, when faced with threat or pain, people often lean into their own oppression. This dynamic, furthermore, while romanticised and enjoyed in our wider culture, is often used to further discredit women who are seen as "weak" for performing a role that they are in many ways set up to play and which, however awful, inevitably takes a sort of strength to endure. Not only is weakness expected of certain groups, but it is then used as a narrative to further discredit them.

While I was writing my thesis, no phenomenon so dramatically or famously typified this masochistic, self-defeating tendency as that of the infamous "Jihadi brides", who were salaciously featured in tabloids at the time.[18] During the rise and fall of ISIS, the Western media became fascinated

18   Circa 2014-2017

by the stories of these young women who gave up their lives in Europe to marry ISIS fighters and bear their children in war-torn Syria and Iraq. From Austrian teenagers to Glaswegian students, they were typically characterised in the press as weak, naïve and misguided.

Sally Jones, known as "the White Widow", was one of the most iconic of the Jihadi brides. Eventually killed in an American drone strike, her death came as no surprise: she had spent the past four years depicting herself as a Romantic figure, always flirting with death for the sake of rebellion (and love). Formerly a beautician and a musician in a punk band, whose father had committed suicide when she was ten and whose first husband had died of cirrhosis of the liver when her first child was only three, Jones' life already had something of the turbulent "Romantic" about it even before she married the teenage ISIS hacker Junaid Hussain. An early recruit, joining her husband and the caliphate with her young son in 2013, she quickly became a symbolic figure. When her young husband died, aged twenty-one, in 2015, her narrative was further romanticised — most often by herself. Her last words on Twitter were: "I'll never marry again. I'll remain loyal to my husband until my last breath."

Sally Jones' life history became a focus for the public relations of ISIS, which Jones herself clearly encouraged. Using numerous Twitter accounts over the years and posing with a Kalashnikov and a pistol in various photoshopped images, Jones helped ISIS put forward the image of a Romantic, noble cause, designed to tempt new followers to convert from Western ideas and expectations of women to those of ISIS. And yet the gendered narratives used to recruit these individuals employed motifs thoroughly entrenched in Western culture. Although the martyrdom narrative used frequently by ISIS has clear precedence in previous political situations such as suicide bombing in Palestine and the Hunger Strikes in Northern Ireland, the self-sacrifice of Jihadi brides (whether or not they die) reveals an awareness of wider cultural tropes. Indeed, the phenomenon of selfless Jihadi brides owes as much to gothic novels like *Dracula* and the idea of the vampire's bride, as it does to a familiarity with religious martyrdom.

The idea of women giving themselves over to dangerous men is a deeply entrenched and popular idea in Western culture, and yet in the context of the supposed submission of women to ISIS fighters, the Western media cast it as a sign of weakness and lack of agency. Whether or not women were indeed "submitting" in this political situation, and on whose terms, there was clearly a double standard in the sense that such behaviour was demonised in this particular context, but not in every other story of women giving themselves up to the bad guy, a typically romanticised and entertaining trope in Western culture.

The idea of romantic self-sacrifice was not the only draw. As Sally Jones was well aware, dressing up as a nun holding a pistol played with motifs as disparate as the slightly gothic adverts for Scottish Widows, images of witches in film and art and even kinky nun outfits. She played the rock star (flirting with death) as well as the groupie, the *femme fatale* as well as the doting wife. This was all in line with ISIS's wider approach to propaganda, which has been rooted in pop culture from the beginning, with persistent appropriation (or subversion) of motifs from Western horror films, particularly.[19]

---

19   See: Simon Parkin, 'How Isis hijacked pop culture, from Hollywood to video games,' in the *Guardian*, 29 January 2016.

The image we see of individuals like Sally Jones is, moreover, an interesting interplay of seemingly clashing narratives about women from both sides, with the Western media tending to depict women radicalised by ISIS as "brainwashed", "seduced" and "victimised", and influencing public opinion accordingly.[20] Either way, these ideas played into a typical stereotype of women as lacking agency due to their gender, and associated "feminine" characteristics as weak, easily seduced, submissive, dependent and unstable.

These narratives that surrounded the so-called Jihadi brides were gendered on both sides and rooted in the same key ideas: the Western media re-ran the story of the passive, seduced victim of the bad, foreign man. ISIS were a little more creative, meanwhile: they subverted Western cultural tropes to persuade women (and men) that there was a better alternative to those familiar Western ways — a Romantic, noble and exciting conversion to a better way of life. It has been estimated that approximately 850 British citizens travelled to Syria and Iraq to support ISIS groups.[21]

The stories on both sides were mostly proven to be delusional ones, however. Whichever way the story is told, what met Jihadi brides was oppression, hardship and often death — from both sides. These individuals, and their fates, neither resembled the image put forward by the Western media, nor that held up by ISIS. Previously, I explained how terrorists are, like other historical villains have been, treated as scapegoats in order to assuage social anxiety following political strife, and Shamima Begum was no different in that sense. However, her particular

---

20   See: Lizzie Dearden, 'How Isis attracts women and girls from Europe with false offer of 'empowerment', in the *Independent*, 5 August 2017.

21   See: 'Who are Britain's Jihadists?' *BBC News Online*, 12 October 2017.

demonisation was heavily gendered. She was depicted in turn as a villain, a victim and a possible figure of redemption. She was played but then she also played back.

While Shamima Begum, along with other Jihadi brides, was depicted as young, naïve and lacking in agency, she was not punished as such. Rather, she was demonised, becoming the ultimate "fallen woman", and othered to the extent that her British citizenship was revoked, meaning she could not even stand trial — a crucial tenet of democratic process. Although many male ISIS members had returned home and kept their citizenship, and sometimes gone on trial, Shamima Begum was made an example of in ways they were not. She was also depicted very differently to Sally Jones, "The White Widow"; she was not glamorised but simply demonised.

She wasn't only a Jihadi bride, after all, she was "other" — of Bangladeshi heritage, which would be used against her when it came to revoking her citizenship. She was also a teenage mother. When two of her children died, sympathy was hard to find, at least from the British government. When her third child caught pneumonia, they were refused asylum or aid, and the baby died. Since then, she attempted to appeal the revoking of her British citizenship, which had left her stateless, but at the time of writing, to no avail. She is therefore in exile — keen to leave the fallen Islamic State, but deprived of citizenship of any country.

She was scapegoated, victimised and objectified all at once, in a heavily gendered, racialised manner, reaffirming these powerful "cautionary tales" about what happens when the "good girl" goes bad or when the "good immigrant" strays. As such, her story epitomises the toxic story of power and control at the heart of Western identity politics. Shamima Begum became a cautionary tale, a modern "fallen woman", a soap opera that millions tuned into, but few protested against. Instead, the audience — the public — consumed the story, as it consumes other stories — passively, unthinkingly, in part because it is so incredibly familiar that any other story seems, perhaps, illogical. She was made an example of, as another fallen woman who personified everything to fear and avoid, even as she was cast out and ridiculed.

Society continues to glamorise and consume this narrative in so many ways, other than the overtly political spectacles — obsessing over "fallen women" and their inability to resist the temptations of men, leading to their inevitably tragic end. Lana Del Rey's characters — for she has played many, over the years — are nearly always a version of this hopelessly romantic victim of an American Stockholm Syndrome. It's never fully clear whether they have true agency — and freedom — or not; instead, there is a flirtation with the sense of being trapped, and of masochism. Lana Del Rey is consistently in love with the baddest boyfriend of them all: America.

In many ways, she — or at least, the characters she plays in her songs — embodies a sort of conflicted white femininity; feeling guilty behind the panes of the country club, in the passenger seat of an Aston Martin, on the leash of the bad man she loves so much. She knows it is bad for her, but she does it anyway. It is a mood, as they say. It is an era that has never left us. It is an eternal masochism — and often faith — that remains, often ambiguously, beyond sense, reason and science. It is Romanticism, dying for love, masochism, self-sacrifice. It is pain. It is love. It is political.

The masochism that Lana Del Rey sings of is a very privileged one; she tells sad stories, without necessarily having to live the reality of the situations her characters are in. She sings of being white trash, endearingly, and it makes her very rich. Are these her sisters? Are we sisters? Class becomes an affectation, something put on and off depending on the track.

This rich, white femininity is confused, stuck in a feeling of precariousness and co-dependency, as well as the guilty privilege of sleeping with the enemy, of never being truly free. It is to experience victimhood and sexism, but also to be attached to the illusory superiority of the past, by association. It is to be scared of solidarity, genuine solidarity, for fear things may get even worse. It is to believe the stories, on some level, the romantic stories about being special and beautiful, and to worry that by losing these illusions, we might lose everything. It is always wanting someone to save us, and yet knowing, reasonably, that we can only save ourselves.

It is to be precarious and fearful, primed for submission, sometimes finding relief in weakness itself. This white femininity bleeds into "white feminism", in which white women struggle to understand where they stand in relation to each other, let alone anyone else. It is to not really trust anyone, even — and perhaps especially — each other. It is to assume that individualism is the only real option, politically, because no one else can be trusted. This identity, this ideology, which has been constructed so that we distrust and compete, is inevitably splintered and precarious. White feminism is a legacy of the "divide and conquer" approach to everyone subordinated by white men, by patriarchy; it is an internalised state of being, a psychological trap and an endemic lack of imagination.

However, merely to dismiss it as such — to flag up "white fragility" — is to miss the point, and also to miss the opportunity for progress. It is important to understand why people feel fragile and under threat, and why they — or we — accept a worldview, ideology and culture that perpetuates it. We all need to challenge this state of anxiety and fragility, but also offer compassion and a way forward that takes into account the individual anxieties, delusions and genuine pain that keeps people in this (sometimes gilded) cage of gaslighting, isolation and fearfulness.

So what keeps people in a state of perpetual exclusion and isolation, fearing solidarity and progress? What keeps people in toxic relationships, whether in a political sense, or in friendships and romantic relationships? How, in these contexts, does fear operate in a way that prevents better lives and communities? Is this really a wider existential crisis, splintered into individual ones?

In moments that are fraught with anxiety and precariousness, people become defensive and avoidant; they cling onto life as it leaves them, desire as it fades, and a glance as it moves to someone else. They are mourning through the spectre of another, or obsessed that if we open our lives to other people, they will hurt us. This fear, this paranoia, exists on every level of society, and it is what sabotages progress and true unity and happiness.

We fear dying and losing those we love. We are scared of a back turning, of nothing else after that, of an abysmal sense of nothingness — of having, and being, nothing. And this — what we fear — is exactly what we are playing out, over and over again, when we get stuck in this paranoid sense of fragility, this Stockholm Syndrome. We invite our fear — our pain, loss, humiliation, guilt — and we play it out, over and over again, at the expense of others and at the expense of ourselves. We only invite the intimacy and love we think we deserve, because we have never been shown that we deserve more. We scorn peace for something more familiar. Many people will shut out other people to avoid being hurt, being vulnerable again. But this avoidance of vulnerability is exactly what makes us fragile. It is exactly what makes our lives precarious. We do, after all, need other people.

This is a typical existential crisis that so many people fall into, regardless of race or gender (but more damaging, typically, when played out by the more powerful and privileged in society against those with less), and it drives many of the social divisions we see today. When we decide to cut ourselves off emotionally from one another, we become individualists, we become atomised from one another. This is also a symptom of liberalism — we become splintered, separated individuals, intent on fulfilling our ambitions as singular people, not as genuinely inclusive communities.

Perhaps this is why Lana Del Rey's music is so compelling: we see the gilded cage, the familiar masochism, but beneath all of this toxic behaviour is a desire to love, to be with other people, as much as it is to be free. It is to be dissatisfied with the modern world, with individualism, just as much as it is to be disillusioned with co-dependency and romance. Whatever the case, Lana Del Rey's music presents the messiness of our modern existential crises, our human weakness, our internalised toxic behaviours. While perhaps we'd do best not to glamorise it all perpetually, we can nevertheless learn something from it being said out loud, admitted, even cried over. From the raw emotion and the eroticism of weakness.

We can progress if we not only admit our fragility, but delve into it, interrogate it and face up to it. Why are we so scared? Do we really not think there is anything out there that is better than how things are now? Dare we dream of something else? Lana, like perhaps so many of us, seems to edge us towards that, however ambiguously, and romantically. But there is still so far to go, and there is a certain weariness, a fatigue, of knowing this and lacking the spirit (for have we not been crushed) to conceive of something better.

To take our power back, to have any hope of real freedom, we have to evolve beyond masochism, politically and personally, which in many ways is a form of escapism and denial about the reality of our own oppression and the fearfulness that affects. But what is surprising about that? When an individual has less power than her partner, for instance, it may seem logical on some level to appease him. Subconsciously, she rejects her reality by living in an illusion that he can change, that he is not so bad, that he does love her, that by staying with him she has more than she would have by herself. She becomes dependent because she is scared of being alone, or what he might do if she left him. Fear, in this instance, conditions a woman to lean into her own subordination, but it is ultimately enabled and justified by structural imbalance.

We should not need to lean in to our own intimidation and subordination; we are more than that, of course. As Dawn Foster so brilliantly explained in her book *Lean Out*, however, only structural change, where women actually have enough power to challenge the abuse and control of the men in their lives, and in politics and business, will really change women's lives for the better, and put them in a position where they can truly demand equality and respect.[22]

It can seem like a Catch-22 situation, though: if you don't have much power (comparatively) to a partner, then it can be difficult to resist them. Some may aspire to have significance by association; by staying close to the more powerful, there is a vicarious sense of importance, perhaps. Or, when faced with a sense of powerlessness that seems impossible to escape, some

---

22   Dawn Foster, *Lean Out*, Repeater Books, 2016.

may find it seems logical to appease the other person or class, either consciously or unconsciously. They may live in denial, as a way of coping with pain and oppression. Or they may find some genuine peace in submission, as Hegel suggested that the "slave" could find transcendence within, despite and then through their physical situation.

Either way, it is understandable why an individual may lean into an abusive or imbalanced situation — an ultimately masochistic, self-defeating dynamic. Faced with pain, why not try to enjoy it and make the most of it? Faced with fear of being alone, why not cling to the person intent on possessing you? Faced with insecurity, why not remain in the one constant thing, a bad relationship? Faced with a chaotic world, why not keep pretending that those in power will fix it one day, that they did not hurt you, but some amorphous "other", not the very people who are supposed to protect you?

Sometimes, others gaslight us. Sometimes, we gaslight ourselves. Either way, we end up a cautionary tale, one more example of weakness, not power or freedom, which can so easily become a self-fulfilling prophecy.

For us to move on and progress, whether as individuals, or in a wider struggle for freedom, equality and respect, it is necessary to face up to the masochism sometimes at the root of self-defeating behaviour, as well as the relative lack of self-worth compared to those who are more powerful and perpetuate that power through intimidation, corruption and a form of widespread, destabilising gaslighting. People stay powerless and self-defeating in their obedience to outdated and misleading structures. It is important to realise, though, that sometimes there is pleasure or at least peace in masochism, or surrender, or acceptance with what we have, rather what we want. Sometimes it's easier to live in a dream created and lived by someone else, to live through someone else more powerful, in order to escape one's own reality. Sometimes masochism and delusion fulfil a need.

Moreover, as Freud, Schopenhauer and Lacan all observed, in different ways, there is an undeniable draw to the dark things in life — to madness, chaos, loss of control, weakness and death itself. Escaping oneself and one's reality through submission to those who are or appear to be more powerful is a human instinct that may seem counter-intuitive and at times tragic, but it is human all the same. I think, at the heart of this, is the desire to accept life as it is, and to accept oneself as one is, and as others tell we are, in search of peace and the disintegration of our own egos. It's a desire to be numb, to be relieved from the anguish of wanting more. It's wanting to believe that bad men are good as they are, that parents, somehow, loved us as they failed us. We betray ourselves out of love, sometimes, out of hope, and out of denial.

Often, masochism is really delusion, if a willing one, or it is a way to appease one's abuser. It is wishing they were someone else. It is wishing away the bad traits, or pretending they are something else. Addiction works similarly: the drug is both the solution promising respite, and a source of shame, a perpetuation of what someone else once told you about yourself. But the hurt is real, and blocking out the fear related to it, or submitting to the threat, or a proxy-threat, or living a lie, is not the solution to truly feeling that original trauma and finding a way to recover from it therein. It is only ever going to be a tonic, a medicine, that alleviates pain but does not heal.

Sometimes, with this in mind, I wonder if masochism is linked to a self-destructive element which does not necessarily want to destroy the self, but to destroy the constructed identity one has been expected to perform, the "gender baggage", and especially the constructed gender role. I wonder if the masochistic cycle is often about becoming aware of this frustration, and simply finding an outlet for it. People are brought up, in Western culture and many others, to fear the feminine; Freud wrote about the buried desire to kill the mother (and separately, the father), and Maggie Nelson writes about the baggage of this idea so evident in Western culture and its cruelty towards mother figures particularly, but also women more generally.[23]

Whether one is embracing the self-destructive role of the fallen woman, or viewing such a figure with scorn or pity, there is a deeply embedded sense of misogyny related to revealing femininity at all, especially the sort that deviates from socially acceptable, "good" femininity. In another way, as the next chapter will show, instances of "failed masculinity", in which men go mad and collapse their own gender role in this way — by descending into "feminine" weakness, emotionality and rash impulsivity — also reaffirm this pattern. Where misogyny belies a wider repression and fear of the "feminine" when it is not neatly stored within certain social conventions, seemingly senseless or reckless attacks on such gender baggage reveal a frustration with these roles and their expectations, and their diversion from reality and truth.

At times, it can seem that masochism is a surrender to what one really wants — whether that is to destroy the identities we perform, or the identities we have been encouraged to expect, or the illusions we have been told are real. It's an attempt, through a sort of brutality or senselessness or self-sabotage, to find some "truth" in being feral or powerless or other — and by that, I mean simply a stating or acting out of what one really wants.

---

23   Maggie Nelson, *The Art of Cruelty: A Reckoning*, W.W. Norton & Company, 2012.

We do not always know why we want what we want. Sometimes the relief is just in expressing desire, and expressing what is not desired, rather than in fulfilling desire itself. The "truth" is just that we desire things we are not supposed to, things that do not necessarily make any sense. Romanticism allows for this world of senselessness, this running into storms, and collapsing into madness, and though Enlightenment thought has defined so much, in regard to the boundaries of sense and culture and how we conceive of politics and our choices in relation to that landscape, we remain emotional, complex creatures, driven by unconscious desires we cannot always understand. Masochism, in my mind, is merely a way of trying to reconcile with what at first glance is a drive towards self-sabotage, but which usually fulfils a real need, or at the very least reveals a buried, often logical conflict within yourself and your relationship to society and its rules.

This instinct can become confused though, and when combined with the processing of trauma, whether personal or intergenerational or communal, it is easy to become lost rather than liberated by this embracing of emotion. In *The Master's Tools Will Never Dismantle the Master's House*, Audre Lorde writes about the need to take back one's erotic power, the energy that exists in black women (especially) but has been manipulated and repressed by white European patriarchal structures over the centuries to disempower and contain. As she so beautifully articulates, "The fear that we cannot grow beyond whatever distortions we may find within ourselves keeps us docile and loyal and obedient, externally defined, and leads us to accept many facets of our oppression as women."[24]

---

24   Audre Lorde, *The Master's Tools Will Never Dismantle The Master's House*, Penguin Classics, 2018.

These "distortions" are the structures placed on us through institutions and socio-political conditioning, and which we are often barely aware of. But it takes not only an awareness of the great emotional power at our disposal, but also our resilience. By owning our own fury, our passion, our love and joy, we prove formidable and triumphant. The challenge, as Lorde writes, is to move beyond the "distortions" that keep us "docile and loyal and obedient". We are not dogs but people. We must recognise the distortions and either reform them or dismantle them entirely.

Watching Our Worlds Burn

As I finished early draft chapters of my thesis, I would wind down watching TV and films, and yet even this seemingly separate activity began to seem irritatingly, inevitably and unavoidably relevant. I'm sure it's common enough that when you study a subject in much depth, you begin to see it everywhere; for me, that subject was not just fearfulness, but the rituals people invented to deal with it, the thinly veiled perversions played out on small screens.

And so, in the evenings, I'd watch things like *Homeland* or *The Sopranos* or *Mad Men*, and there they were again — broken, often abusive, powerful men, doing bad things and then eventually paying their dues or unravelling in some way — from Tony Soprano in *The Sopranos*, Brody in *Homeland*, and Don Draper in *Mad Men*, I was clearly not alone in being drawn to these ambiguous, complex, flawed men, watching their gradual downfall (and often their redemption, however fleeting) with fascination.

To watch the fragile masculinity of (at first glance) very powerful men shatter could be cathartic, and even subversive. Literature and drama were full of these anti-heroes and their unravelling, from *King Lear* and *Hamlet* to *Macbeth*, from Edgar Allen Poe's abusive protagonist in *The Black Cat* to the most contemporary political figures. And as these characters unravelled, so dramatic in their moral failure, I couldn't help but notice that this ritual was one of mourning, in part. These stories and spectacles facilitated a compulsive mourning of the masculine, its breaking apart, its weakness, and really, the impossibility of this performance beyond performance itself.

The rise and fall of Donald Trump, meanwhile, turned political spectacle into a Shakespearean drama, with this Lear-like president descending into madness and bringing his desperate followers and family with him, storming the Capitol mid-pandemic, for instance, on a dramatic winter's afternoon. The punishment of terrorists and enemy dictators fulfilled a similar function — whether a dishevelled Saddam Hussein being probed and prodded by military doctors, or court illustrations of Abu Hamza in prison clothes behind the dock, or Harvey Weinstein or R Kelly led into court — there was often a strange catharsis to be found, presumably, in the spectacle of a once-powerful man's fall from grace, the drawn-out destruction of flawed men. But did these performances subvert patriarchal structures or simply reinforce them with a conflicted, masochistic nostalgia and the repeated replaying of communal (and personal) trauma bonds in which compassion, desire and self-destruction coalesced?

In *Mad Men*, the charming and distant enigma, Don Draper, unravels routinely — haunted by his secret childhood of poverty and cruelty, through his adulthood of extra-marital affairs, day drinking and emotional unavailability. Though he never entirely spirals out of control, at least not permanently, the extent of his weakness and unhappiness is barely seen by anyone in the show itself, only the audience. We get to find out what makes him tick — something no one in his life really does. In *The Sopranos*, meanwhile, the murderous mafia boss Tony Soprano makes his confessions to his therapist, but never tells her everything, so again, it is only really the audience who can grasp the full picture of his character and faults. In *Homeland*, Carrie pursues the prisoner-of-war-turned-traitor-

and-terrorist, Brody, but only as she falls in love with him. She needs him to unravel, for the sake of her country, but his clever elusiveness, their psychosexual cat-and-mouse game, triggers her own extreme unravelling. They dance and mirror one another, as the series goes on, both patriots and both liars, their shadow-sides only visible to one another, in an extended falling apart, a compulsive rampage of destruction, as they on the face of it try to stop it.

All of these performances and plays, whether contemporary or classic, real or fictional, reveal the fallibility and humanity of those who seem all-powerful, in a way that allows the audience to gain access to characters who are inaccessible in real-life situations. The "distant father" figure may not be actually approachable or transformed, in his character, but he is visible, and perhaps this is compelling to so many viewers because being able to see and better understand the "distant father" escapes them in real life. Moreover, to see these usually powerful, detached men collapse under the weight of their own mistakes and repressed emotion is satisfying and even cathartic.

In showing these weaknesses, these shows also undermine the gender norms that these patriarchal figures typically represent, even as they make dangerous and chaotic men sympathetic to some degree, for failing and so subverting their own performed masculinity. Following a Romantic, Gothic tradition, these characters, and the shows and plays that feature them, reveal the emotional depths and complexities of seemingly unreachable men, and their behaviour in the world. In so doing, they are both a transgression of Enlightenment values and an expression of fear of the "failed" sexualities and genders that they are concerned with. Although the shows and stories mentioned create iconic characters, they do so through exploring the link between gender and morality, and how it defines what we are expected to be versus what we really are (not only beyond masculine and feminine, but beyond good and evil). It's an exploration of "who we really are" and who people around us really are, which is itself scary. Western society, and many others, remains terrified of what happens when gender roles and the moral values associated with each one are collapsed — what happens when Don Draper or Tony Soprano loses his nerve — and these shows provide both a cautionary tale and a cathartic playing out of what we already, however subconsciously know, about the people these characters remind us of.

When I watched shows or read books about catastrophic male characters, I felt comforted, but I could not always work out why. I felt a sense of warmth for these characters, even when they fell apart, or perhaps especially when they did. I loved them for their weakness, or for showing it. I could watch them from afar, and connect to fictional father figures, imagining for a moment that I understood them and knew them, as I might have known my own father.

And yet I also wondered if this was entirely healthy. Was this simply indulging a part of myself that was attached to an illusion or distant memory of a father figure, in the absence of a real one? In a wider sense, do these cathartic dramas about flawed men give us a way to exonerate the real patriarchal figures in our lives, who we are scared of and confused by, in a way that is nostalgic and a form of wish-fulfilment, without offering any real route to healing or justice? Do we watch consequences play out in fictional works, for fictional father figures, so we do not actually have to confront our own?

—

In *The Black Cat*, a classic of the horror genre, a man gets drunk and starts lashing out first at his pets, and then, eventually, his wife. He confesses these transgressions not in the hope of swinging the verdict on his crimes, but to unburden himself, perhaps even to "make sense of" what seems to him, in many ways, unconscionable. He wasn't himself, he says. That behaviour was "not like him".[25] One is reminded of the tabloid profiles of certain young, white men after they have committed atrocities — "like any other father" (about a man who murdered his daughter for going out), "a sweet child" (turned fascist mass-murderer), "a loving husband" (countless abusers). Although aggression and dominance are widely attributed to ideas of masculinity, to become an insane murderer is usually considered not only toxic, but in some ways beyond masculinity. To lose one's sense of reality, to become reactive, emotional and mad, is to swing too far into the realm of "feminine" characteristics.

And so instances of domestic violence, and alcoholism for that matter, present a problem for those who seek to firmly establish gender binaries; a man who has become so paranoid and delirious as to harm those in his domestic sphere, whether a wife, children or pets, has collapsed the gender binaries that established stability in the family home. His falling apart is a challenge to gender binaries and also the Enlightenment notions behind any equation of masculinity with rationality. This is why madness, possession and rage are explained away as a fleeting thing — the doing of a demon, somehow — not really the man himself. To admit otherwise would be to concede that his masculinity is fragile, a house of cards. And so

---

25   Edgar Allen Poe, "The Black Cat" in *The Portable Edgar Allen Poe*, Penguin Classics, 2006, p.192.

the black cat, in this story, becomes the convenient scapegoat, the demon who explains the evil we cannot attribute easily to ourselves (or to men). In other stories, perhaps the wife would fill this role — or the "other woman" — but Poe, writing in the 1800s, made it more palatable and also more esoteric than that.

The narrator in *The Black Cat* is, he insists, a rational man. While he blames "Fiend Intemperance" — the devil drink — for allowing his soul to become so weak as to be possessed by violent madness, the narrator's concern seems to be his own propensity to transform as he does so, and to be so different from that which he understands his identity to revolve around. The drink is a catalyst, but it cannot explain everything. He does not even blame it entirely. He blames a *cat*. He is convinced, even as he knows it makes no sense, that a cat has driven him to murder. Here we have the fiction and impossibility at the heart of Western thought: our rational selves require irrational "others"; men project their insanity, chaos and monstrosity so that they don't have to admit it in themselves. Their suppressed "feminine" characteristics transform into everything they fear of femininity — Madness! Sin! Submission! — only projected onto something else, whether a cat or another person.

Femininity here is entangled with Poe's notion of "instinct" and irrationality, and their relation to one another. In drawing us into all this confusion — should we believe that the narrator has been possessed by a cat? What of his story is "real"? — Poe enacts his own sort of "demonic" possession of the reader. For a moment, our own understanding of reality may be suspended, confused. Poe challenges, therefore, "the hegemony of human reason"[26] simply through writing this story. Echoing the insights of his previous essay, "Instinct vs. Reason: a Black Cat", where he wrote that "the boundary between instinct and reason is of a very shadowy nature", in this story he uses an account of a man's transformation from "rational" to "mad" to reveal the fragility of our own grasp of reason on a conceptual as well as personal level. He reveals that "instinct" and "reason" often collapse into one another, that instinct is a form of intelligence. Certainly, possessing a reasonable nature does not necessarily require a refutation of "instinct".

Related to this, accepting rather than expunging "the feminine" may prove the key to a more stable personality, one could argue (and perhaps Poe does). Although *The Black Cat* would seem to imply, on one level, that by losing his mind, a man also loses his masculinity: "when a man loses his mind, he is losing his manhood as well,"[27] in collapsing into feminine cliché of being submissive, weak and delirious, this only happens because the narrator refuses to consider that his original actions could betray his own implicit, human weakness. By suppressing an awareness of his weakness (as a man), he becomes convinced something exterior to his own personality has caused "the insanity", and so he actually spirals into madness and confusion. The pressure to be "a man" — a rational man — knocks him into the strange logic that a cat must have provoked him, rather than his own volatility, his difficulty with the drink.

There is a chilling motif of blinding, which resembles certain

---

26   Clark T. Moreland and Karime Rodriguez: *The Edgar Allan Poe Review*, Vol. 16, No. 2 (Autumn 2015), 204-220.

27   Ibid.

well-known scenes in *King Lear*. In this famous presentation of the old king's descent into insanity, but also truth, he only truly "sees" when his actual eyesight has been destroyed. His own daughter, Cordelia, must transform (effectively) into the loyal Fool, or court jester, to be able to communicate anything honest. Likewise, perhaps, only when our narrator has blinded the cat — who is really a projection of himself — does he begin to see his own, now damned, truth. Sadly, as he seems to lose his mind, he comes to his senses in some way — gradually seeing the error of his ways and admitting his violent alcoholism. When he destroys his wife, he becomes the (toxic) feminine — submissive (to the cat), weak and crazy. "Superstitious", as he noted that she had been.

In so doing, this story encapsulated the fears of many men in Poe's time, that accepting and following the rules of gender binaries — and the Enlightenment — would not prevent one's fall. This is a story of a collapse of the domestic sphere; a sort of "Adam and Eve" of Victorian times. The poison, the demonic animal... It is a familiar tale. Some would place this story alongside Poe's "temperance tales"[28] — moralistic and anti-alcohol — and certainly there is a streak of the cautionary. But I would think that Poe only uses this familiar trope to tell another, more terrifying story — something that would torment his audience far more than prospect of "the devil drink" alone.

This is a story where the ultimate horror is that being "a real man" is a fiction. The narrator, or story, is our own "black cat" — it is the space onto which we may project our greatest fears about what we truly are. And it is not just a man or a woman; it is a sprawling confusion of sense and instinct, masculinity

28   James Hutchisson, *Poe*, Jackson: University Press of Mississippi, 2005.

and femininity, learned behaviours and the unpredictable unconscious, the desires we don't understand, or even know, and cannot, at times, control. We are wild things and yet this still comes as a surprise. We train one another to be docile, tamed wolves turned into pets, and yet, out of nowhere, a howl, a bite, a disturbing dream.

In this vein, Poe took inspiration from Fuseli's painting *The Nightmare* (1790-1).[29] Poe's narrator describes his drunkenness as if it is a sort of sleep — a delirium, anyway — and portrays the black cat similarly to Fuseli's incubus, complete with staring, domineering, reckoning eyes.[30] The demon is the narrator's, perhaps also the artist's mirror, as is the submissive human they torment in both works. In this split personality, and in this disturbing dream made public, we see a fight between Enlightenment and Romantic values, where Poe and Fuseli both ultimately reveal that we are made up of both, and cannot rid ourselves of either. Poe's narrator finds some sort of truth, some self-reckoning, in his delirium (as well as damnation); Fuseli's repressed desires, the unrequited infatuation that drove him to torment, became something beautiful and true in being articulated as they are in this painting. A sense of the sublime influences both gothic works.[31]

Poe captures the horror of personal transformation in this story, and in so much of his work, revealing how fluid, fleeting — indeed, mortal — we are. The death of masculinity, the

---

29 Christopher Frayling, "Fuseli's The Nightmare: Somewhere between the Sublime and the Ridiculous," in *Gothic Nightmares: Fuseli, Blake, and the Romantic Imagination*, London: Tate Publishing, 2006, 9.

30 See the *Preface* for an illustration and discussion of Fuselli's painting.

31 See Barbara Cantalupo: *Poe and the Visual Arts*, Penn State University Press, 2014.

fracturing of the self, the cataclysmic triggering of violence by alcohol — Poe's portrait of a man come undone is also archetypal of these related, and more recent treatments of distant, powerful men who unravel. Beneath our fascination with such figures is a desire to deconstruct masculinity and the façade of one's reasonable self itself, and all that it conceals; it is a desire to give into the sublime and the storm.

This is related to masochism, in the sense that self-sabotage, repeated in ritualistic cycles, can be a form of finding one's "truth" or the truth about people close to us — about letting the subconscious speak and demand, however senseless it seems. There is relief in that alone, however self-destructive or senseless it may seem to an outsider or even the subject themselves. To embrace what is terrifying can seem masochistic, and perhaps is still masochistic, but it is also simply a way of reconciling with a terrifying and incomprehensible world.

> Bold, overwhelming, and, as it were, threatening rocks, thunderclouds piled up the vault of heaven, borne along with flashes and peals, volcanoes in all their violence of destruction, hurricanes leaving desolation in their track, the boundless ocean rising with rebellious force, the high power of resistance of trifling moment in comparison with their might. But, provided our own position is secure, their aspect is all the more attractive for its fearfulness; and we readily call these objects sublime, because they raise the forces of the soul above the height of vulgar commonplace, and discover within us a power of resistance of quite another kind, which

gives us courage to be able to measure ourselves
against the seeming omnipotence of nature.[32]

Such Romantic ideas about the Sublime, such as this passage
by Kant, can help further explain this mentality, and this drive,
I think — why we want to let ourselves go, and let others go,
and accept ourselves and one another as they are. As Kant
wrote, overcoming fear causes delight, or "a deliverance
from danger"; there is a palpable sense of joy at escape and
relief alone. He also explained that the sublime arouses a
"negative desire" in people that both attracts and repels.[33] As
he articulated so well: "The experience of the Sublime is one
of almost being crushed. Our powers of imagination break
down, and all that remains is an admiration or awesome
respect of something immense."[34]

So is there a strength in being weakened, in submitting
to the overwhelming, awe-inspiring chaos of the world
and minds we live in? Is there at least some pragmatic or
psychological benefit to it? In her book *Hurts So Good: The
Science and Culture of Pain on Purpose*, Leigh Cowart explores
the pleasure of pain, and in particular the way in which the
nervous system responds to pain with painkillers which are
pleasurable in their own right.[35] In this sense, more pain can

32   Immanuel Kant, *Kritikk av dommekraften*, trans. Espen Hammer, Oslo,
      1995, 118, quoted in Lars Svenden, *A Philosophy of Fear*, London:
      Reaktion Books, 2009, 80.

33   Ibid.

34   Rainer Maria Rilke, *Duineser Elegien*, Munich, 1997, quoted in Lars
      Svenden, *A Philosophy of Fear*, London: Reaktion Books, 2009, 79.

35   Leigh Cowart, *Hurts So Good: The Science and Culture of Pain on Purpose*,
      PublicAffairs (2021).

lead to more pleasure, or at least a pleasurable relief of the original pain. It's a trade-off, in a way, that acknowledges and uses the body's underlying chemical processes to control a reaction. Whether or not this behaviour is learned or innate and universal still remains unclear, and is probably a mixture of both. As I mentioned previously, existence itself, for many people, can give enough trauma or uncomplicated pain to lay the foundations for one to develop a masochistic relationship with it. If not universal as such, then chasing pain for the pleasure wrapped up in it, for these neurochemical reactions, or moments of distraction, is common enough.

In *The Sweet Spot: The Pleasures of Suffering and the Search for Meaning*, development psychologist Paul Bloom looks beyond masochism to understand why humans continually embrace or persist with behaviour that hurts them. "A lot of the negative experiences we pursue don't provide happiness or positive feelings in any simple sense — but we seek them out anyway", he points out.[36] There is no obvious, instant "neurochemical" benefit to many cases of human suffering that humans nevertheless continue to endure. And yet, they do not give up. However tragic and absurd this may prove — think of the *Myth of Sisyphus*, in which Sisyphus is doomed to merrily roll a massive rock up a hill, only for it to roll down again, for eternity, as an illustration of this point — humans continue with their optimistic, doomed struggle.

Bloom suggests that our stubbornness is rooted in the search for meaning, and the deep-seated belief that there is indeed growth and progress to be found in the most complex and difficult experiences, whether planned or passive events.

---

36   Paul Bloom, *The Sweet Spot: The Pleasures of Suffering and the Search for Meaning,* Ecco Books, 2021.

Happiness is not the only goal, or even the top goal, of human efforts. People want fulfilment, but that may require suffering and difficulty. As he puts it, "Some degree of misery and suffering is essential to a rich and meaningful life". While this does not exactly explain why people would specifically chase pain and self-destruction, it reveals that people have other desires beyond pleasure or even material security or shelter or safety. People are searching — for meaning, or their own freedom to be "themselves", or to find another way to be, or to feel chaotic, even, to break down what they have been taught so far. Humans are experimental, they are thrill-seekers, and they know that they will die — so nothing is off the cards.

Humans are also weak. Whatever Nietzsche says about the slave morality, and however much he criticises its tenets, he knows that it brings comfort to people who need it, helps nurture the "inner life" of contemplation and compassion, and he knows that the approach is one chosen by many, in any age, as well as a worldview experienced by those without any other options or freedoms. Oppression remains a reality still; humans are adaptable and find ways to survive it and to have meaningful lives, despite everything. My favourite passage in Corinthians displays the sort of attitude Nietzsche may have loathed, but in many ways it also reminds me of his own writing, his particular atmosphere, or angst:

> My grace is sufficient for thee, for my power is made perfect in weakness. Therefore I will boast all the more gladly about my weaknesses, so that Christ's power may rest on me. That is why, for Christ's sake, I delight in weaknesses, in insults, in hardships, in persecutions, in difficulties. For when I am weak, then I am strong. I have made

> a fool of myself, but you drove me to it. I ought
> to have been commended by you, for I am not
> in the least inferior to the "super-apostles", even
> though I am nothing. — *2 Corinthians 12.*

This line, "I have made a fool of myself, but you drove me to it", can seem almost comical. Perhaps Nietzsche would never have said such a thing; perhaps it's exactly what he would have said. The sense I get is that Nietzsche knew we are as weak as we are strong, though not all so in equal measure, but importantly that humanity is defined by this struggle, this desire for meaning and love and connection and resilience — this hunger — and so often the failure of those efforts for fulfilment.

Nietzsche wrote his immense works of philosophy as one conjures a storm; he was transgressive and ingenious. He wrote about transcending society but never denying life. In this sense, I think he must have understood the draw to reconcile with human frailty, with our own failures, even as he gave ways to build something beyond ourselves entirely. If any philosopher embraced human weakness and still found meaning in its suffering, it was Nietzsche, however much it maddened him.

Nietzsche also wrote about pleasure and the Sublime at a world perishing,[37] in a way that reminds me of some Christian Armageddon enthusiasts who look forward to Judgement Day. Are humans, on a deep level, actually primed (and priming one another) for death? For the end of it all, or rather just our own

---

37   Friedrich Nietzsche, *Nachgelassene Fragmente 1884-1885,* in *Kritische Studienausgabe,* vol. xi, (Munich, Berlin and New York, 1988), 267-8, quoted in *A Philosophy of Fear,* 83.

end in such an immense, incomprehensible and excessively beautiful world? Do we like — and need — to know we are so small in something so grand and impossible? Whether there is a God or not, do we not need to be reminded of our place in the world — small, weak and foolish? Do we not all, at certain points, want to cry out, "For when I am weak, then I am strong. I have made a fool of myself, but you drove me to it"? There is truth in this existential rage, in its heaven and its void. It is human nature to experience it and to wrestle with it. Life is inherently threatening; we could all die at any moment. There are so many ways in which people jostle with this existential crisis — emotional reactions that engineer ways to escape reality, briefly, and create at least the illusion of power that might negate that state of mind, whether it is through finding power oneself, at the expense of others or vicariously through others, and at the expense of oneself.

Religion is perhaps the most obvious way in which people take steps to make peace with the Fear they feel in life and of life; it offers solace through the reassurance that there is a higher power, that we do not have real control, but that it doesn't matter because God does, and God has your best interests at heart. Political leaders — and even romantic partners — may say similar things, though the nature of their intentions may vary. Ultimately, though, we are social creatures, and find in these relationships — whether with God and other religious followers, or through political or social relationships — ways to alleviate ourselves of the crushing paralysis and alienation of the Fear.

When people find themselves in the turmoil of addiction, for instance, AA or NA present the same structure of thinking. By surrendering to a higher power, people are given a way to divert from the fight-or-flight response that triggers substance abuse and those repetitive, compulsive cycles. By embracing one's powerlessness, and therefore one's vulnerability, there is the potential to deal with fearfulness and anxiety very differently.

In similar ways, I found, art can also provide emotional solace, camaraderie and meaning, that reassures and negates this fearfulness. It can offer a way into acknowledging one's vulnerability and human weakness, and that of others; it allows the emotional barriers to be removed and communication lines to be opened. It allows for a form of love and spirituality that is not dissimilar from the practices and ideals of religion. At least, this is what occurred to me the longer I spent time with my father; it was art, more than anything, that gave his life meaning and assuaged his greatest fears. Art helped him feel loved, in the end.

—

After my father's fall, and as we spent more time together again, I came across the work of the sociologist Thomas A. Scheff, on catharsis, drama and psychological healing. The idea of explicitly using catharsis as a means of psychological therapy had first been proposed by Sigmund Freud and his colleague Josef Breuer, who studied it in relation to hysteria in their patients, creating a treatment based on catharsis. To Freud and Breuer, catharsis meant the venting of built-up aggression in therapy, which they proposed would have the short-term effect of alleviating that sense of aggression. However, they later abandoned this use of catharsis as a therapy, moving on to develop psychoanalysis, "in which emphasis is placed on conscious insight,"[38] and which the pair considered more likely to bring about permanent change in their patients as opposed to transient relief.

According to Scheff, however, Freud and Breuer were premature to give up on the idea of using catharsis to heal individuals. Developing a theory of catharsis developed from both the aesthetic and psychological traditions, Scheff argued that "the evidence upon which Freud based his judgment that cathartic cures were not permanent now seems unconvincing".[39] Scheff developed his idea of therapeutic catharsis, affected through giving the audience or patients (depending on the application in healing, ritual or drama) an "aesthetic distance" with which they could safely process accumulated or repressed anxiety without becoming overwhelmed:

> At aesthetic distance, the members of the audience become emotionally involved in the drama, but not to the point where they forget that they are also observers. Aesthetic distance may be defined as the simultaneous and equal experience of being both participant and observer.[40]

Catharsis, to Scheff, was the effect of a process such as a ritual, play or therapy situation, in which members of a social group are given an aesthetic distance whereby they are able to experience a confrontation and release of anxiety. The process

---

38   Thomas A. Scheff, *Catharsis in Healing, Ritual and Drama*, University of California Press, 1979, 20.

39   Ibid., 44.

40   Ibid., 57-59

relied on there being a structured set up that facilitated this aesthetic distance, as well as a group of people with whom to share this process, which was essentially a communal one focused on shared anxiety. As he put it: "I… propose a theory of ritual and its associated myth as dramatic forms for coping with universal emotional distress".[41] Drama therefore had the ability, and was perhaps predicated on this mechanism, to relieve or purge anxiety, affecting this particular emotional and aesthetic phenomenon of catharsis.

These ideas resonated with me deeply. While it was clear to me that societies used rituals and drama to assuage communal anxiety after political trauma, often in a violent way — and I would go on to write about this in my thesis — I also witnessed it closer to home, albeit a more peaceful version. Talking therapy was not for everyone, after all, and I had seen that first hand. I had tried for months to get my father to talk, and these efforts seemed futile. He was still guarded and detached, and averse to talking. I would ask him probing questions, using the interview techniques I had picked up as part of my course, and yet he remained quiet, laughing off any serious discussion, or any discussion at all. The idea of undertaking psychotherapy or psychoanalysis was impossible for him.

Around this time, however, he started asking me to go to the movies with him. This was not something we had ever done before, but it quickly became a routine. We'd see light comedies, usually, but one day he said he wanted to see the recent adaptation of *Anna Karenina* directed by Joe Wright. I had always been drawn to *Anna Karenina*, but the strength and depth of my father's own connection didn't fully cross my mind until one scene, halfway through: Anna trying to visit

---

41 Ibid., 108.

the son she had left, after she had left her husband to pursue an affair and was therefore ostracised from her family and wider society. Of course, I realised all at once, seeing the soft light of the film glaze over his face, he felt like the little boy in *Anna Karenina.*

He wasn't speaking, but he was sharing, in a subtle way. A dark-haired woman who had an affair, who lost her son as a result, who was addicted to opiates, who took her own life. She might as well have been his mother. I looked at my father's face and he gave nothing away, as usual, and I looked back at the screen. But he was sharing something with me, then, in his way. Taking me to the pictures was the closest I would ever get to him telling me about his own past, the one he could perhaps not even fully remember. Fiction filled that impossible void; he let me in, at a distance. Trauma, mediated through a screen.

I couldn't help but connect this experience, and my father's wider behaviours, to Scheff's insights into catharsis and aesthetic distance as crucial components in individual and communal healing after trauma. I came to understand how sharing stories through watching and reading them together can provide the aesthetic distance necessary to process repressed trauma, which is not accessible or possible for everyone. Conventional talking therapies require the patient to talk in depth about one's feelings and buried anxieties, and my father barely talked at all. Repression was so entrenched in his upbringing. But *Anna Karenina* enabled him to heal and communicate without having to talk at all. It gave him the aesthetic distance to come to terms with his past and ultimately to share it. I like to imagine it lifted his burden a little.

It wasn't until my father died, about six months later, that I found out more about his mother, when I discovered a notebook he had written in, with an outline and some vignettes in which he sketched out a plan for novel about his parents. Family relatives, at the same time, shared details that had been kept back before. His mother had died on her fifth wedding anniversary, in London, having overdosed on codeine and whiskey. She had been having an affair with a Polish officer and had fallen pregnant, it was said. In those days, that was a hopeless position to be in. The pieces began to slot together; my father's pain so clear, so crystallised.

He had never been able to reconcile why she had left him at such a young age, and he had never been given the opportunity or freedom to talk about his own emotions and searing sense of abandonment. Though his grief and despair was obvious in his long silences, his barely veiled depression, nevertheless it was repressed, for him. He was trapped by an inability to talk. And yet, *Anna Karenina* became a way for him to understand his mother, and feel, through the vicarious sadness of a character in a novel who so resembled her, the emotions he had been forced to contain entirely on his own. It also became a way for me to understand him, eventually, and a way for him to let me in. He couldn't talk but he could read and watch; perhaps, for him, this was enough. It was certainly all he could manage — the form of healing and reckoning with his own past that he felt safe and able to pursue. And so, without talking, but with *Anna Karenina*, we had come to understand one another.

After a lifetime of living with this trauma, watching a similar story play out on screen helped him heal in a safe way, in an activity that was ritualistic. He needed that distance to confront the loss of his mother, and the neglect he had experienced as a child. He needed to see a made-up story because he did not know enough about her, and could not believe the rumours he had heard. The cinema became like a hypnosis, in which he could tune into the grief below the surface of his thoughts and habitual numbness, articulated by someone else who had also understood.

As the stories about powerful, distant men unravelling had given me a chance to come to terms with the failure of masculinity, and the way in which societal expectations of masculinity had caused a chasm between my father and I, his obsession with *Anna Karenina* also betrayed a desire to see the "failed femininity" of his own mother. She had not done what was expected of her; she had had an affair, succumbed to her own addiction and despair, and left two children without a mother as a result. She was hidden away even in death, because her family were ashamed of her; she had failed at being a wife and mother in society's eyes. But she had still been there, and she had been human, despite her death and erasure. By reading and watching *Anna Karenina*, I think, or hope, that my father was also able to see beyond those narratives of failure, shame, gender and simplistic moralism to see the person beneath — a tragic figure, but also, always, his mother, whom he loved eternally.

I'm not sure he was ever able to fully heal from the trauma of her death. When I was younger I never understood why he was always so numb and detached, so spaced out. Now, having experienced similar states, and spent time with him towards the end of his life, I realise he was traumatised, that the Fear accompanied him persistently, and this disassociation was a flight-or-fight response that was part of that emotional reality. By watching films, reading books and going to exhibitions, he was able to find another sort of relief from his emotional crisis.

Still Lives

The day before my father died, I went to see an exhibition of photographs by Robert Mapplethorpe at the Grand Palais in Paris with my boyfriend. At that time, I had been living in Paris, subletting short-term from my old landlord, and we were in a long-distance relationship. I was also going back and forth to Scotland a lot, for my course and to see my dad. We'd spend time in museums and cafes, when he was around, stretching out our free tickets and expensive espressos, to fill the frozen, bright days.

We went to the exhibition in the morning, which I was reviewing for a magazine. I knew my dad was ill, but I didn't know quite how bad things were. There had been so many scares before that I had begun to not really believe it could ever happen. I was waiting to find out whether I needed to book flights back, though, whether it could really be that bad, when we went.

It was a strange time. We walked around, trying to be normal, but death loomed anyway; a stark crow in the otherwise green and pristine Luxembourg Gardens; window displays of eerie candles and flower arrangements. I tried to concentrate on work — I was trying to get as much finished as I could in case I had to leave Paris — but even my work was all about death, it turned out.

We took the Metro from Montmartre to the Grand Palais, an imposing building surrounded by decorative gardens and busy roads, and random police marching around. It was eerie and dark inside, like a mausoleum. Women in veils and latex, dying flowers and bowed heads. Fur and lipstick and Irish hair, props and faces lit to seem as blank as sculptures from Ancient Greece. A large white, minimal cross on the wall, next to all the other crucifixes and dying roses. A figure in a blank hood.

There were Polaroids that Mapplethorpe had taken in the 1970s and formal black-and-white portraits of the artist and his friends. He had created a system of iconography that embraced S&M and Catholicism at once, in this pursuit of true beauty. There were classical, sculptural nudes and arrangements of flowers. "I am looking for perfection in form", he was quoted as having said, his words on the wall of the museum. "I do that with portraits. I do it with cocks. I do it with flowers."[1] He lined up Saints and rent-boys, celebrities and Michelangelo. Striving for transcendence, perfection and immortality, he had developed an aesthetic, spiritual code in these figures, flowers and icons. He had re-appropriated religious iconography to show how art and sex were his own religion. He had written a letter to Patti Smith: "I stand naked when I draw. God holds my hand and we sing together".[42] There was Robert and a skull, Robert in drag. Robert with a cigarette. Robert living with/dying from AIDS.

But his photographs betrayed none of these struggles. Instead, they were an altar to his idols and ideals, beyond good and evil, beauty and ugliness, success and failure. He had used art to transcend, to go beyond struggle and fear, to assert his own ideals in spite of the doubt he must have felt or experienced from other people, and the fear of his own they betrayed. By transforming images of death, sex and himself so that he triumphed, transcendent and by turning what seemed pornographic into a form in the language of

---

42   Patti Smith, *Just Kids*, Ecco Press, 2010.

Michelangelo, he sought redemption not only from personal, spiritual dilemmas, but from life itself, and the fear of death that implied.

The nudes are so still, I wrote down, sitting on a bench in front of them, *that they cannot be alive and, of course, frozen in time and a photograph, they are not. The flowers seem to be placed as carefully as funeral arrangements. The little altar, with images of Jesus' crucifixion, together with the lines and lines of photographs of Mapplethorpe's friends and idols, complete the reconstruction of a fantastical funeral. He has reconciled with doubt, pain and death; he has created his own meticulously executed send-off.*

We walked out of the exhibition, out of the darkness. Outside, the pond shone turquoise and shallow, with statues and tourists in the distance, and a froth of fine algae at the bottom. I sat on a chair by the pond and smiled and smiled, and my boyfriend took a picture of me. We were both wearing black, and my skull scarf flickered against my skin in the breeze. I had not picked out these things intentionally.

After being in such dim light before, I was surprised by the brightness of the sun outside, the fresh green of the gardens and trees we walked through, after the soft tones of marble and spot-lit flesh and bone. We walked on to the Jardins des Luxembourg, where the pathways were covered in fine cream gravel. I heard a strange noise as we walked that I couldn't quite place — a lone cry — and looked around to see what it was. I saw a single black crow, seeming oblivious to the people straying around, standing still on a spot of the lawn, continuing to make its odd, eerie cry, beak open, towards the sky. "Isn't that creepy?" I said, and my boyfriend nodded and we kept walking. It had seemed so incongruous there, in the green and the sun, as tourists in neutral travel clothes wandered around nearby.

We had just come back from the Mapplethorpe exhibition when my mother phoned and told me how bad things were. "He's not getting better", she said. I had been so used to being told he was dying that it didn't seem fully possible as a reality. But I booked flights to Scotland for the next day, anyway, in a daze. By the time we got home, he was gone.

—

There was a nervous atmosphere at home, with people sitting around, waiting for the funeral to happen. Death seemed unexpectedly public; everyone knew about it. He had been ill for such a long time, during which we had often been ignored or looked down on as a family, mainly because financial problems had followed illness so swiftly.

He had, to me, died very slowly and gradually, and detached from the outside world. The grief was therefore dispersed over the years, but no one had seemed very involved until this point, in which he had physically gone, which seemed in some ways quite arbitrary. I wasn't sure how I felt about it entirely, but at times it felt good that I was finally allowed to be proud of him, to tell people what he was like, to be allowed the ritual of death. The illness had become a strange spectre, before — haunting us all with the imminence of death, the Fear — but now that tension faded, and in a strange way it brought him back to me, more fully, in essence. A spirit distilled, managed, sort of. As if grief can be bottled, memories saved, legacies controlled.

In the week or so before the funeral, so many flowers were delivered that they took up every surface: lilies, their scent pervading over every other, white roses of various shapes and arrangements. They covered everything: a large dinner table, side tables, sideboards, a dresser, two desks. They arrived in cellophane and paper, with sad notes from friends. So much white, but occasionally some purple, from a thistle, the dark green stalks and long, winding leaves. When all the vases were used up, I found other things, jugs and glasses, to put them in. We bought a couple more vases as well. I took most of the leaves off the stems, cut them down, arranged them between the vases.

As the days went on, I plucked out the dead ones as they wilted, rearranged the bouquets with those flowers missing, merging them together. Cutting stalks, refilling water, bundling all of the cellophane and ribbons into rubbish bins. There was so much clearing up, cutting things away. I thought of Mapplethorpe, the flowers he had photographed. I imagined the actual process that had gone into them. How many flowers had he bought, for a photograph of one? What did all the waste look like, scattered around his studio? What did he do with the leftover flowers, and the flowers he'd finished photographing, when he was done with them? Or did he just discard them, decadently, or busily, efficiently, entirely focused on the art at the end? Why had he not photographed more dead flowers, decaying things, why this stark purity?

I thought of those flowers again — his entwined white tulips and star-like orchids and sensual, begging lilies. The dark and light, the harmony and yet the desire, pushing through. I thought of them over and over, as they flickered in my mind, and somehow, it quietened my despair.

A lot of the flowers had already started to wilt by the time of the funeral, which was later than usual because Easter had made the church's schedule busy. The service itself was to be in the afternoon, but the cremation, which was to be more private, was in the morning. I went with my mother, aunt and uncle in a black car over the Tay to Dundee. The crematorium was in a part of the city I hadn't been before, in a well-kept garden surrounded by grey stone tenements on the hill.

I went with my mother inside and we sat near the aisle, on the left. I noticed the coffin, placed on the altar, raised up. The priest gave a short service, the words of which passed over me as I kept looking at the patterns of colour on his robes so I would not look at the coffin.

I held her hand as he sunk beneath the ground to be burned in a chamber. It seemed like some sombre magic spell — a clunky disappearing act. So strange, I kept thinking, that there were only moments between his body being there, solid and still, and then gone to ashes. A lever pulled, it sounded like it, a steel door open and then shut, a measured fall, a letting down. A camera shutter, shut. A man, gone. A man down.

The funeral service itself was in a church in St Andrews, later that day, around the corner from the Scores, where we had briefly lived, and yards from where my father had spent his summers with his grandparents, swimming in the large, stone outdoor pool that held a pit of icy blue ocean and many children, in those days. It is still there; with every tide, a new swimming pool, now empty.

I sat with my two sisters and my mother to my left. We had all worn our hair down and we were all wearing black — new clothes that shone in the tinted light through the windows. I looked around, briefly, noticing a crowd of mostly familiar people, though more aged than I had seen them last. A few were prominent for their being estranged before. Tailored black suits and navy twin sets, shiny shoes. An all-pervading cloud of incense from a previous service, sticking to the soft grey walls of the church. A choir, standing awkwardly, respectfully. Rows of quiet people.

Later on, in the library of a hotel, looking out onto the perilous North Sea, we had a small Wake. I ordered several bottles of champagne, and someone else brought some of the food left over from the gathering immediately after the service — triangular sandwiches and homemade baking. A waiter — French, brunette, and stern — kept topping up glasses as the mood gradually soured. People made small talk tiredly;

the Swedish cousins lightened the mood when they arrived, wearing white rather than black, never seeming to age.

They talked about mutual ancestors, one of which, Sir Patrick Spens, had died in a shipwreck, so an old ballad went,[43] and I thought about them at the bottom of the sea, bones now gone to sand, washing up with the tide. I had never quite appreciated before how much we were from this place, generations playing on the beach and dying nearby, centuries of them. The mythological and the immediate, in the poetry and ice of the sea. As I thought of the ancestral links, however, I felt detached from them too. Who were these people, anyway? Who was my father? What did any of it really mean — family? Sometimes it was far easier to feel a connection to a distant legend than a direct relative.

Later on, we went up to our hotel room, which I had booked before, so that we could have some privacy and not have to worry about going home at the end of the day. By the time we went up, the mood had plummeted. I was so tired, but it had billowed into despair, something I couldn't sleep with. I fixated on the alienation and the emptiness. I felt entirely alone in my mood as I locked myself in the bathroom. I started running a bath and took a sleeping pill, watching the bubbles form under the water, gushing from the tap. I slipped out of a white towel robe, feeling a broken mess, feeling angry, trying to meditate on the water and the sound it made, but wanting to drown in it. I was tired of tears and other people. I dreamt of another life, without realising that I was already on the edge of it.

Over the next few days, the last of the cut flowers died off

---

43   *The Ballad of Sir Patrick Spens*, one of the Child Ballads, of anonymous Scottish origin.

and were discarded, and the place felt emptier for it. I couldn't take it all in at once, so I began just taking photographs of them. Robert Mapplethorpe took me by the hand, and perhaps my father did too — gave me lilies and roses, morbid confetti. I tried to capture the flowers before they died. I drew each one, recording their gradual wilting, as they flopped and fell. After I had taken so many, I put the photographs away, hid them, and tried to live.

I found out I was pregnant days later. In mere weeks, the last days of my father's sickness were replaced by the overwhelming and insistent nausea of early pregnancy. In nine months, funeral bouquets were replaced by congratulatory "new baby" flowers. The natural cycle renewed itself so efficiently, from a full moon to a new moon, just like that.

Bodies broke and reformed, grew; ashes scattered. Many seasons passed. The flowers stayed frozen in their short lifecycles, on a desktop, ignored. My new love transformed everything.

Anatomy Lessons

At twelve weeks pregnant, I lay back on the hard, padded examination bed, light grey-blue, on a paper sheet, with my stomach bare. Not showing yet, thinner than before from all the sickness. I'd been living on occasional slices of toast and tea and little else. Even the vitamins made me throw up. Now I heard the heartbeat I had been so anxious to hear — a busy murmur of life, magnified. It was as if I, too, had been brought to life, after years adrift. I couldn't look away from the screen, from the *pump, pump, pump* of a soon-to-be-baby. I couldn't really see it, but there was life in there, now. Before he knew a thing, before he felt a thing. Squirming with a pulse and his needs. The love felt in a rhythm, for that's what he was first — a rhythm, a beat, faster than my own.

Later, I pored over the pictures from those scans, in blurry black and white — at the sweet little nose and clenched fingers, at the smooth profile of his forehead. I kept imagining what he would look like in the world, in my arms. But I couldn't. He was this mysterious, amorphous thing; barely a weight, yet.

Month by month, he grew — we grew — into a weight, though. By the winter, I was already carrying him in my arms, though he hadn't been born yet. My own skin did not seem strong enough; as I walked in the ice, I felt him kicking me, turning his hips, punching anything I rested against. I waited.

We waited. My boyfriend came back in the evenings, after work, when I was nearly asleep.

—

Just as I had photographed flowers when my father died, I photographed my bare, swelling stomach as my son grew into life. I tried to connect to myself, too, but I found that harder. My body seemed, now, to have a life of its own that my mind could not fathom at all. It was busy and vital and in control. It was vulnerable but I could not quite reach it. I could not console or assuage its nausea, fear and pain.

Grief and pregnancy interweaved so physically that at times they seemed the same process, too. As the days and weeks went on, I felt increasingly wiped out, and I wasn't entirely sure how much of it I could attribute to the tiny new life sapping me of energy, and how much was the effect of grief. I found myself too exhausted to think very much, and so everything became immediate and physical, and so harder to disentangle and discern. Everything had changed, that was all that was clear.

My boyfriend sent me reassuring messages and emails, though, which helped bring me back into some sense of myself, helped wake me up from the in-between world. Between surges of panic, nausea and terror, there would be flashes of bright, soft love. Messages that said he would see me soon, that everything would be OK. *Everything will be fine, I'll make sure of it,* he wrote. *Our baby will be beautiful.*

I had booked into an early ultrasound because I was anxious to know that it was really happening. I heard the heartbeat I had been so desperate to hear — a busy murmur of life, magnified. On hearing that sound, it was as if I, too, had been brought to life, after years adrift in a netherworld. A mass on an ultrasound, once a cause for devastation, my father's tumours on a screen, was now a cause for celebration.

And yet, for all the joy I felt, these moments seemed haunted. As the morning sickness began, I would remember how I had woken to the sound of vomiting only a couple of months ago. The pressure of the past and the growing future seemed at times to be suffocating, and so overwhelmingly physical, so that my mind almost struggled to exist within it. I had become a body, but not just my body. It was someone else's body now. It was not altogether unpleasant — merely surreal, dislocating and strange. Submission for new life. Fading into a season.

As we got closer to the due date in late December, I went back and forth to the doctors. There were so many tests — the tubes of blood and measuring of the ever-growing bump, the recording of so many obscure facts in a growing wad of medical notes, which I was told to carry around with me to every appointment. I felt like a student again, being lectured to and always slightly out of the loop, fearing childbirth like an exam I could not prepare for.

The days grew shorter and the streets iced up. I collected baby clothes and nappies and lotions and little hats. I bought a Moses basket and placed it on my side of the bed, anticipating a little creature sleeping near me soon. And yet I could not really imagine him at all — I was so rooted in the present, in pregnancy, that this near future seemed at once miraculous and impossible.

—

I didn't show, really, until I was about six months along. The first few months, especially, had been so all-consuming that it was constantly so confusing, that there was no visible "evidence" of this new condition. It was a secret.

Even after the bump was visible, though, people didn't see it. I once walked up and down a train full of men in business suits, at eight months pregnant, and no one offered me a seat. I went to the end of the carriage, where the toilet was, and saw another pregnant woman who had also missed out on a seat, but had found a pull-down seat there instead. She pointed to another one; I pulled it down and sat down there instead. Visibility was not inevitable, no matter how obvious we were; other people chose whether or not they would see us.

—

In mid-December, I began to suffer from a collection of symptoms, including tachycardia and very high blood pressure, that usually signalled pre-eclampsia, a serious condition that could be fatal and so meant hospitalisation. After a day of tests and medication, I was wheeled into the post-natal ward, because there were not enough beds in the antenatal ward. This meant that as well as the beeps of machines and the wheeling of trolleys, there were the high-pitched cries of newborns, swaddled by their mothers or sleeping in the tiny plastic cribs.

I had been nervous of coming here, to the hospital my father had died in earlier in the year. I had been back twice before for scans, but only as an outpatient. This ward was far more similar to the side of the hospital I had experienced before: the same layout (although with those additional little cribs) and very similar views. I was put in a bed by the window, and as I looked outside I remembered that my father had been in a similar position, although looking out of the window on his right rather than his left. His bed had the view of a helipad; I had watched as an air ambulance had landed, as he lay there, gaunt and barely conscious.

The sky darkened much sooner now than it had then. He had been in hospital for a first bout of pneumonia the year before he died, in May. Now, only two weeks away from the winter solstice, it fell dark before four in the afternoon. As I lay in bed, hoping that the medication I had been given would work, I watched the drizzly rain outside, darkening into a night dotted with amber and white and occasional ambulance lights. I could hear the sound of someone else's baby on the CTG — a fast little heartbeat as she waited to be born. As the evening wore on, I began hearing more newborns, their crying that sounded more like the bleating of lambs, strangely soft and small and sweet.

My eyes began to sting, though, feet hurting and heart jittery, head tired from the heat of the ward and a day of questions, a day of memories. My racing heart was deeply uncomfortable, and gave what would have been a stressful experience anyway an added level of anxiety. The memories kept coming back — the flashbacks to sitting on the window ledge of another ward, trying not to impose on the other five men on the ward, whose relatives were not there, and who were so ill that they could not draw their own curtains or even ask for their privacy.

My dad had been delirious and red with tachycardia, hardly able to function. When he was still at home I had given him medication for the dehydration and water, not realising how serious it was at the time. He deteriorated so quickly; but then he bounced back. I don't know why I was surprised: until he died, that was his usual thing, as if he was tricking us and tricking life, escaping death. It was always so hard to tell, though.

Having seemed so out of it the whole visit, my father had surprised me with how lucid he seemed when he blew me a kiss on my way out. It was very hard not to cry. I waited until I was outside. I had thought, then, that he was kissing me goodbye.

When he actually died, I had missed that moment, though in his last phone call to me he had said, "I love you" in a weakened voice. It had caught me off-guard, but I said, "I love you too". That was it. It echoed through this time.

The other babies on the ward continued their first cries, some tentative and some rather more assertive. I looked at the large baby bump, seeing him wriggle beneath my skin, his little feet and hips jutting out occasionally. He seemed well enough, I was glad to see. I was tired though, and none of these babies were. I found it hard to sleep, and barely did so at all that night. Whether it was my heart rate or the medication or the babies or the lights. I couldn't stop thinking about the pain and boredom and worry my dad must have gone through in a place like this — with its bleached atmosphere of tepid lights and flesh-coloured curtains.

Had he wanted me to know that this is really what it was like? When he looked at me deliriously, his heart racing, his life — maybe, maybe not — slipping away? There had been just one look, right before he blew me a kiss goodbye, that convinced me that he did. That after all the secrecy and pride and pretending things were fine, in that moment of being vulnerable and letting me see the pain he was in — the physical, mental, existential anguish — he let me in. I love you, I remembered again. *I love you.*

—

A few weeks later, the sun woke me, or so I thought. I was lying on my side, the only way I could lie, my arm around the bump. As I woke, I shielded my eyes from the light, which was dulled only slightly by the condensation on the windows. Blurry, sleepy, but with a vague sense of adrenaline that I couldn't place, I got up and went to the bathroom. Every day of the past few months, I'd been going every hour, round the clock, the baby pressing against my bladder.

It was New Year's Day, and so, so still, as I walked through, past my boyfriend asleep in white sheets, his black hair stark against the pillow. We had stayed up the night before and drank a single glass of red wine (I was allowed that, apparently). I checked my watch, now — it had just gone 9am. Weirdly punctual to begin the year like that, I thought. Unlike me, in fact.

I sat down and my waters broke — just like that. As if waiting for the cue. *A punctual baby. A New Year's baby. 9am. Really?* But there was no mistaking it, even though I had never gone into labour before. I had never had a baby before. I didn't know what it felt like, and yet: *now I do.* This bit, anyway. The knowing before I knew it.

Waters breaking, but nothing felt broken or different, really. No "breaking", just water. On and on and on. And yet, imperceptibly, my body had been taken over entirely. It decided when and where, I saw that now. We had to trust it, both of us. And at least it was punctual, as if aware of the symbolism of its physical turns. As if this had been marked on a calendar all along. New Year's Day. *New Year, New Me.* New you.

My heart thudded; I rubbed my eyes. *It's happening.* It didn't stop. I thought of him — my tiny, heavy, kicking thing. A little boy, or so they said, from the ultrasound. *There's no mistaking it.*

"How will we know it's our waters breaking though?" Someone had asked in antenatal class.

Oh you'll know." We all looked unsure, but accepted it nonetheless, like we had to accept everything, in our apparently endless ignorance. "In any case," the midwife had said, "it's unusual your waters would break. Only 10 per cent of births begin that way." I was relieved, as I remembered that — that I knew it was happening, that there was no doubt. No wondering if I was in labour. Just a surreal certainty. In labour, sitting there. Everyone else asleep, but not us.

Everything was happening, and yet I couldn't stand up. I sat there for a while, baby heavy in my pelvis, laying in a nest of muscles and organs, head almost resting on my lap, but not quite. I felt him, holding the bump, hoping he was OK. This boy I'd never met, but through touch, mere skin between us. My skin and blood, my own.

I heard my boyfriend wake, call my name. I was nervous to say it — to put into words what we had been waiting for, for so long. In the emptiness, the New Year's silence, for the first words to be: "my waters have broken". Echoing from the bathroom, unsure.

He smiled when I came back into the bedroom, though, and after the initial excitement and nervousness, the strangeness of more waiting begins. Towels? Is the bag ready? Should we call the hospital? Not yet, but quite soon, because they told us to before. "I'll phone them in a bit", I said, trying to settle into the time scale, a rhythm that was beyond me. I looked out of the steamed-up window, at the streets below, entirely empty, grey with melted ice and dew.

He made breakfast, as the pain began subtly, and I phoned the hospital. "OK, you should come in then. You know where we are." My bag was ready, but I checked it again anyway.

Towels, baby clothes (enough for four days), scratch mitts, a baby hat, a blanket, a change of clothes, underwear, dry shampoo, normal shampoo, make-up... We ate eggs and toast at a round white table in near silence. Nervous, probably. I was nervous of the impending pain; he was nervous of seeing it, I think.

I packed the bags and made my way down the grey hard steps and out into the cobbled street. The shimmering Tay and a play park, bare trees, cold cars parked along the road.

Approaching the hospital in the still January air, I tried not to think about the oddness of it, the weirdness of having been here nine months ago to pick up my father's death certificate. I had accompanied my mother into the hospital, where she talked to a group of four nurses standing in reception, who had vaguely known him, in the eighteen years he had been in and out of hospital. The bureaucratic processes of death seemed surreal to me, as they handed over an official piece of paper, folded up — a record of the event of his death, which I had missed by a day.

Arriving at the hospital now, my own medical notes were in my bag — a wad of forms and diagrams and instructions. Birth and death both required a paper trail — a stark elegy to a physical process. Ordinary things. Reduced to paper, to notes and forms and these brief sentences, simple facts betraying nothing.

He had died in the spring, at the end of March, in the year that had ended hours ago. A pregnancy separated then and now: a vast and unpredictable condition, a thumping little body beneath my skin, wriggling and moving in the night, but quite still now. Asleep, as all this was happening? His head resting in my pelvis, cradled within.

I stepped carefully out of the car. There was no one around. There was ice in the air. We walked together into the hospital, my boyfriend carrying a large bag. All of the shops — the newsagent, the hairdresser, the café — were shut.

We went into the maternity triage unit, also empty except for two nurses on duty. They smiled and took details; we took our place in a room, awaiting inspection and judgment. I lay down on the bed, looking at the bump, round under a white top, holding it with my hand by default, and wondering how long the labour would be. I didn't know what to expect; I was too tired to keep imagining what could lie ahead. I closed my eyes, which had started to tingle and itch, remembering lying alone on a white bed in Paris nine months ago to calm myself. My friend Laura had asked to take my picture for a series she was working on called *Another November*. Each month in a year — a year of Novembers, following a break-up — illustrated a different moment in her recovery. I was supposed to be the last one, the last November. I was the part where she had recovered, on the precipice of something new, something beautiful, some other new, fresh life.

Light had streamed in through the windows, softened only slightly by the white cotton curtains, which fell in folds over the bed. It was spring at last, and sunny enough to wear nothing. The light glowed on my skin and through the swathes of fabric. I couldn't help smiling, even though there was no one to smile to. I was in love with a city and the ideas of things, with a future stretching out.

I was twenty-six. I didn't know that I was pregnant yet, but when I found out weeks later, I always thought back to that moment, which had seemed so sublime, and decided, in my mind, that in some way, it had all begun then — that moment on the cusp of life and death. A brief time when I forgot my worries about my father, and I stopped missing my boyfriend, and I was entirely content by myself.

I had some sense that everything was as it should be, despite everything — that something had started, aligned, relaxed. It was only an instinct — abstract, vague — but it had grounded me then and it grounded me now. That everything I needed, I had. That life did not align for me; I aligned for it.

Eight months later, here I lay, or sat — half-sat — on a hospital bed, as a nurse inspected me, with my legs, already feeling limp with the pain, spread and resting on grey footrests. A paper towel over me "for privacy" — or, rather, so that I couldn't see what she was looking at. So that I didn't know there was no privacy. I wouldn't have been able to look anyway; the bump meant I could barely see her head, her black hair in a ponytail peering in. She stretched and looked around this elastic painful thing — my body, or what had once been mine.

Maybe it never had been, though; this idea of ownership only seeming illusory in moments like this, however, when others prodded and stretched and measured and looked. When another life moved within, small hips pushing against muscles and organs grown for it, just it (or him). A vessel, again, lying here — either coming in to shore, or heading for a rock, it could never be sure until it happened.

"Well your waters have broken", she said.

"I know", I replied. Did she really think I could have been mistaken? Could I have got it wrong? But I was only the ignorant mother-to-be, not qualified yet to know anything. Would I get a certificate when I was done, to say I knew my own body now?

"But you're not quite far enough along yet." She went on. "For pain relief. You could go home—"

As she kept speaking, stern and listless, the pain swelled again, like roots in the earth bringing me under its surface, deeper each time. But it didn't matter to her how much it hurt, or how long it lasted, or how paralysing it was. I wasn't screaming quite enough. I wasn't dilated quite enough. They couldn't stretch me far enough yet.

I imagined going home — to that cold flat, with no heating other than three small portable heaters, to a shower that wasn't working properly and the grey stone stairs up and down, streaks of paint marking the grey walls. I tried to imagine even climbing the stairs, and I just couldn't. I tried to imagine making it back to the hospital again afterwards, when the first journey had seemed so precarious. I needed this nurse I had only just met, I realised, crushingly. No matter how detached she was, how much she wanted to free up a bed for an hour or two. I needed to be here, I just knew it. She knew as well as I did that I had been in with complications only days ago — or had she not read the notes? Did they care so little? I barely had the energy to speak; the pain paralysed my voice. Where was his anger when I needed it? Where was the fury and indignance when I needed to be fought for, when I couldn't move or speak for pain?

I looked at the nurse, as I was crouched over with pain, as I tried to leave the ward. I physically couldn't, though. What difference did a centimetre make? Could she not see the pain? Was I just the space I'd take on a bed as I bled this child out?

"You can go back in", she said coldly, and then looked away, back at her notes, her screen, her names and numbers and the time on the clock. I wanted to cry but I couldn't. All energy for protestation or expression or relief at small victories was blocked. I edged towards a bed, sickness rising.

—

There weren't enough beds on the labour ward or the birthing centre, so I was put on another, more public ward instead. While there were curtains round my bed, I could hear all the other patients and they could hear me. At visiting hour, I could also hear their entire extended families, crowding around a beloved newborn. During one contraction, when I begged for the nurse, I saw two young girls peering through the curtains, concerned. I closed my eyes and said nothing more, so as not to scare them from ever having children.

The nurses weren't available, and for many, many hours I didn't see a single medical professional, despite frequent requests through my partner. I tried to find more strength within, waiting through the swelling waves, not sure if I was losing or finding myself in the relentless rhythm. I had read a book about learning to submit and go with the pain, let the labour become me, but I couldn't do it. The only way I could deal with the pain was to bring myself up to its strength — somewhere between a fight and a dance, a duel and a duet. I felt as though it would break me if I did anything else. I danced and fought, immobile, for twelve hours. Nothing changed.

It worried me that no one checked that we were OK. No one seemed to believe the pain I was in, because I wasn't screaming. But not screaming was my way of coping. I had no energy to scream, because all of my energy was focussed on surviving it, on not falling apart entirely.

Only at nightfall did a midwife come in, and believe me. She said I could grip on her hand as strongly as I wanted, to show how much pain I was in, and I did. I saw a little flicker of my pain in her eyes. I felt bad for it, but she had got the message. At that point, having been in labour for fourteen hours, she nodded. "We'll get you some gas and air. There isn't any here, but we'll find some."

A little later, the midwife wheeled in a massive gas canister, which looked like it had been there since the 1950s. I quickly inhaled the entire contents. When they finally checked me again, I was eight cm. "She'll be done in an hour, I think," one said to another, as they wheeled me away, like a loaf of bread slid back in an oven to turn a golden brown, rise a little higher.

I was wheeled into a room on the labour ward and slid onto a large bed. There was a little sound system, but there didn't seem to be any way of controlling what played. It seemed to be a playlist of songs that someone had thought would console people. At one point, it started playing "Everybody Hurts" by R.E.M. This was easily one of the most irritating moments of the whole experience: did R.E.M really know anything about pain? Had R.E.M ever been in labour? No. Sadly I didn't have the energy to smash the radio.

As time went on, the pain began to tire me, made worse by the playlist of awful music. The gas and air dulled it a little, but really it just gave me something to do, a way to control my breathing, rather than having much effect on the pain (or music) itself. Although the midwives had thought that I would have had the baby by now, things seemed to have slowed down. I was stuck on the precipice of birth, and it hurt. They still didn't seem to take that seriously though, because I still wasn't making any noise. I was spending every moment I had concentrating on breathing in as much gas and air as I could, regardless of its weakness.

"Oh you don't *look* like you need diamorphine, you're doing so well!" A midwife said. "Very dignified!" I wished I wasn't. Wished I wasn't silent, passive-seeming, even at this moment, dragged out, in impossible pain. I had been built not to complain. I was more like my father than I thought.

"But I do," I tried to say, though it came out as a whisper. My boyfriend spoke up for me this time, knowing how much I had been needing pain relief all day, how worn down I was. "She does," he said, "she does want pain relief. She looks like she's not in much pain, but she is." They looked disappointed, but administered it anyway — a little injection I couldn't feel, a little silvery wave to take my mind off the larger one corroding my spirit. I relaxed and closed my eyes, and as they ran tests, I barely noticed. The music faded, too. *Diamorphine.* A life-saver, or sanity-saver, or spirit-saver. *Diamorphine.* I heard the Velvet Underground, I heard "Golden Brown"; R.E.M. thankfully faded away.

Hours went by, and I couldn't hear the midwives talking or even the baby's heartbeat on the machine as they tied me to wires and tubes. Eventually, unfortunately, the good wave receded; as the pain swelled up with fresh intensity, I could barely move.

"The baby is in the wrong position," they said, "but hopefully we can move him around in the next hour or so." It was the early hours now, dark blue outside with occasional glows of light from ambulances.

As the pain worsened, I could also see that the midwives became less relaxed, less able to give a timespan. Every slight movement hurt unbearably. They began talking about "interventions" if the baby was in distress. Vacuums, forceps, surgery. Tools, instruments, more force. My body was no longer my own.

"It's really too late for an epidural," the anaesthetist said, despite my having been asking for one for twelve hours now. They were understaffed, and she had been busy in surgery, so I had missed my window apparently. "You're ready to push, but he's in the wrong position. If you can sit very, very still, then I can give you one. But it's really too late."

I sat upright, during the constant contractions, as one midwife supported me and the anaesthetist covered a patch over my spine with iodine. I kept trying to be very, very still, remembering what the diamorphine had felt like, even though it wasn't there, to relax me. I remembered being about five or six, in the summer at home in Fife. We used to go to a quiet beach near our house, and while our dad sat on the sand, we'd go into the water. It was always freezing, so I'd pretend I was in the Caribbean, and as my legs went numb I was convinced that it had worked — I'd somehow made the pain go away just by thinking it away.

As the anaesthetist injected the epidural into my spinal cord, the pain vanished. They helped me back onto the bed, where I lay on my side and closed my eyes. Numb was good; I had come back.

I pushed for an hour, and did everything they told me to do, but nothing happened. "You're doing so well, just another one," the midwife said, but it didn't work. He was in the wrong position. The miracle of his sudden change, his movement, didn't happen. A sense of failure and anxiety began to rise up; nothing I was doing was working.

"He's in the wrong position," they kept saying. And then, at last: "We can't keep going." "It's too dangerous. The baby is in distress." A doctor came in, then. First the vacuum, as my legs were spread, and I kept focussed on his expressions: concentration, worry, then a shake of the head. "We'll have to go into surgery," he said. "The baby's in distress. The heartbeat is falling."

The heartbeat.

"This doesn't look good."

Within seconds, they produced a consent form. I could barely read it and I could barely hold the pen, but I signed it. "CS1." It said. "Risk to the life of the mother or child."

Suddenly there were lots more people, a change in atmosphere — action. A small army, mobilised in seconds. They topped up the epidural with something else. "It's a good thing we did this before," the anaesthetist said. "We'd be pushed for time otherwise."

I was lying back, as the people moved around me, transforming into their green scrubs and masks over their faces and white over their hair. The pain was gone, but now acute fear replaced it with horrific, piercing intensity. The concern on their faces, the rising heartbeat, the baby in distress. "This doesn't look good."

I closed my eyes to the swirl of movement around me, as they moved me into theatre. There were now twelve people around me. I heard and didn't hear some names. There were no windows, and a lot of green clothes and spotlights, as if I had landed on another planet and these aliens were quickly inspecting me. They cut me open then, though of course I couldn't feel it.

I closed my eyes and felt my own heart racing; dark memories pushed themselves into my mind as the room went quiet, but for instructions I didn't understand. Back to London, when I was nineteen. Numb with the cold, but not numb enough. A night that had played itself back to me many times in the past seven years, and which never got less upsetting.

A pain that removed everything else like a bright light bleaching out the colours from my vision. I had felt as if I was not there anymore. That moment became this one; the threat became one amorphous, eclipsing void.

When I started crying, the anaesthetist handed me a tissue. "It's OK," she said. She had brown hair and brown eyes, must have been about my age. "It'll be over soon." I wiped my eyes with the tissue. "Thank you."

"Your baby! That's your baby crying." I had not heard it, or I hadn't believed it, stuck in this weird dream, the anaesthetist holding my hand. It was as if my hearing switched back on — I heard the scream. It was so different than what I had imagined, even though I didn't think I had imagined anything particular.

"That's your baby," she said again.

"Can I hold him?" I asked, unable to see him because I was still lying down, having my abdomen stitched back together.

"Not until you're sitting up," she said, "but here," and they passed him to his father. "What does he look like?" He didn't answer me. "Can I see him?"

"His hands are covering his face." I found myself imagining him again, as I had when I was pregnant, but I still couldn't. I could just see that he was big, for a new born. "Nine pounds, five ounces." A midwife said. "He's a big baby, and you're quite small aren't you?" It was bizarre, even without seeing him properly, to think that I had been carrying this huge baby for so long — this huge baby with the huge voice, covering his face from the world he had just entered.

As the surgeons were still stitching me up, half the team abruptly left. "There's a shift change now," the anaesthetist said. "But don't worry, everything will be fine. This is James, he's also an anaesthetist." I looked up and said hello. He shook my hand and introduced himself politely. "I'm James," he said. It seemed a strange way to meet somebody. I saw a glimpse of his face, upside down. Fair hair, blue-grey eyes, kind. "Hi," I replied. He smiled. It seemed funny that the hand-holding and smiles of the anaesthetists had consoled me almost as much as the actual pain relief.

As they stitched me up, James kept holding my hand and smiling in a consoling way. I kept asking what the baby looked like, trying to see him, only inches from me, but unable to see his face because of the huge hat they had put on him, and because he had covered his face with his two hands.

When the surgeons had finished stitching me back together, we were wheeled out of theatre and taken to a ward nearby. There was still a Christmas tree on the ward, with red and gold baubles, and one other mother and her new baby. I was still lying down, but kept asking to hold the baby anyway. "Well OK, for a moment, but you can't sit up."

"OK", I said, and they handed him to me. He was wrapped in a blanket, and quiet now. Our skin touched for a moment — his soft cheek against my hand. He was relaxed, he was alive, he was real. As I held him, it was as if we floated in a dream, as if time could just disappear.

The nurse arrived with a tray of tea, coffee and toast. She took the baby again and put him in a plastic crib. I hadn't eaten in twenty-four hours, and coffee and toast became this transformative, sacred thing. I kept looking at the baby, as my strength returned, lying there so serenely. He seemed almost intimidating in his quietude. Just gazing around, dreamily and formidably. As if he could deal with this, he could deal with anything. In my weakest, most exhausted moment, it felt as though he gave me strength, not the other way around. Every moment with him, I felt physically and mentally stronger.

I had been worried that we would not bond properly, having been separated, but when we were being wheeled up to the post-natal ward, he started crying and the nurse put him in my arms. Immediately, he stopped crying and looked up at me, and I knew then that everything was fine. He needed me too, and I could look after him. We were meant for one another. This whole nightmare had brought us together.

As the hours went on, we bonded tiredly, recovering from the birth. Later, the baby's eyes peered over at me from his crib, watching me silently as the other babies screamed all around us. When he started crying, I stretched over, though I was not really supposed to because of the surgery, and picked him up. He fell asleep on my chest, and then I fell asleep too. The past was gone, the past was here, in one small child's new face.

A week later, after a few days in hospital, never sleeping beyond that first, drugged up rest, immediately after surgery, I received a letter in the post. The latest document in my paper trail. *"Congratulations on the birth of your baby, Baby Spens, born by CS1, risk to the life of mother and child."*

It was too fragile, always too fragile, so risky, this life, but here we were. Nine months ago there had been a death certificate, and now there was a birth certificate. Ships in the night.

I looked down at him — we'd still not named him — another document to sign, a word to choose — and how to choose the right words?

But here he was. Eyes peering up, mouth latching on to my breast. *Baby.*

All that, one word. *Baby.*

After flowers for death, there were flowers for birth. White roses were replaced by pink and yellow and purple. My eyes kept settling on an orchid as the baby fed from me every two hours, as I fell into a daze — exhausted, half-there, though fully consumed by my love for him. As he fed, as my energy depleted, I fixed my gaze on the flowers, as if in meditation, as if their life force would seep into my own.

—

The days were short when the baby was newborn. It didn't really get light until about 8.30am, and then it was dark again at four in the afternoon, so it felt as though we were hibernating. The baby seemed to grow longer every day, as his eyes opened wider, his dark hair became fuller and he became more curious and expressive. He was so serene and attached to me with such natural affection that it was hard to remember how I had ever been alone, how I had ever lived life before him.

I nestled him minute after minute and hour after hour and showered him with kisses. These were the kisses I'd been waiting for. This was love — real love. It wasn't just an escape, a way of obscuring deeper hurt. It wasn't death or grief or even simply human. It was life itself; it was light. It was beyond human. Love like no other. Absolute and yet liberating. I imagined him growing into a person with his own ideas and demands and it seemed the ultimate honour — to be able to bring someone up so that he could be his own person — to help him take his freedom and enjoy life every day.

He didn't like the Moses basket; that became clear pretty quickly. He always wanted to sleep on my chest; nothing else would do. I tended to let him, and then carefully placed him into the Moses basket when he was asleep, but sometimes I fell asleep with him, and awoke to his cries two hours later, just under my chin.

I changed the baby's nappy about twelve times a day. I breastfed him every two hours, day and night. I bathed him in a yellow plastic bath, which he rebelled against at first, splashing powerfully with his angry little arms and legs, outraged. I wrapped him up in a small white towel, held him closely, and he calmed down again. I kissed his little forehead. I took pictures, so many pictures, and when he finally went to sleep, and even though I was exhausted, I missed him, and I would look over them all again, in love with this little person, and his new moments — trying to remember and savour each one, before he grew again, his face changing and his legs longer, his expressions transforming into new.

Sometimes he tried to eat my nose, or nuzzled into my neck and arms and chest. He made gurgling, hungry little noises, a baby animal. Breast-feeding made me ravenous; I ate a KitKat and a bottle of water with every feed, but still all the weight was gone in two weeks, and I was small and thinner than before. That was how hungry and growing he was. I physically lost a third of my weight in a few weeks. It seemed so surreal to just physically disappear like that.

He smiled in his sleep. He liked the sad songs I played him at night, because I thought they might be soothing. Elliot Smith — what was I thinking? But he liked them, to be played on a loop.

When I played him "Between the Bars", I started to cry, though. The old life was over. That's what I imagined my boyfriend thought. That he was missing the old life and he didn't love me anymore. I cried and cried. He told me I was being stupid to even think that way. Of course that wasn't true, he said.

"Baby Blues," the midwife said. "It's very normal. A hormonal dip. You'll probably be fine, it's very normal, but do tell us if you're not."

—

Every day we walked, usually about three miles altogether. Sometimes I carried him, but as he got heavier I took the pram some days as well, so that he could sleep in that while I had a coffee somewhere in town.

Usually we went to a gallery, and he would sleep spread-eagled, his bottom lip pouting and his chin turned up. He fed lots and all the time, refused a bottle. I didn't know a single person there, apart from a curator, who would come and chat to us sometimes.

It snowed when the baby was only a few days old, and I took him out to the park, where tiny flakes fell on his nose, though he didn't appear to notice.

—

It took a long time to heal from the surgery. In the early days, I had to inject myself with antibiotics every day, and pull the caesarean stitches out myself because the midwife, not the kindest woman, told me to. My hands were jittery from the sleep deprivation, but she seemed to think I could do this part myself anyway. "I'm away on holiday next week," she said cheerfully. "Can't wait to get away from all this."

We didn't have a bath in the flat, but each day I tried to steal time for a shower, if the baby was sleeping in the morning. It was always rushed, always anxious, that he might wake while I was in another room, and be terrified.

As he got a little older, sometimes I took him in with me, let the water fall over us both. He would always try and breastfeed, though, at the same time, cradled by my chest. It already seemed crazy to think I had ever carried him inside me. This huge, hungry thing. My skin, where he had been, was soft and strange. I was soft and strange, trying to put myself back together. But I had lost something, lost some kind of strength, even though, on the face of it, I was stronger than ever.

—

When he was five weeks old, we took the baby to an exhibition called *Visions of Void: Florian and Michael Quistrebert.* I stood there with a glass of wine and we laughed, that he was so little and here we were, both in the world again. To not be in bed, to not be in the house.

I walked into the gallery and there were videos, dark backgrounds with licking green flames, on one screen, and pink on another. Yellow on another one, psychedelic flames, that began to look like flower petals turning in on each other. Screens made up of ruched fake chrome metals, its light reflecting on it like solid velvet or satin. Tiny lights like distant planets. In another video, an aggressive optical film, patterns and flickering, chaos.

I escaped the sleep deprivation to see my nightmares on the gallery walls, a "sensory experience"; the baby slept through.

I walked out of the gallery room, hot and sleepy. I kissed the sleeping baby's beautiful little head, feeling out of place and yet not wanting to leave, not wanting to go home just yet. Confused though, because I was tired. I was too tired. He kept sleeping.

—

Around six weeks, things began to spiral. I had lost all that weight so quickly, had barely slept at all since the birth. There was no babysitting, barely any visits from family and friends, and no break of even twenty minutes, at any point, for myself.

I ran on adrenaline for those weeks, I think, and then I got very sick.

First my body had had enough. I developed some mysterious infection related to the surgery and they gave me more antibiotics again, which also made me feel sick. My fever ran so high I start hallucinating and sweating, terrified I wouldn't be able to care for the baby. I ended up in hospital in the middle of the night, where they ran tests again. They put the baby in a crib, and I wished I could have the same crib at home. He seemed to tolerate it better than the Moses basket.

I got better, over the next week, but it was still hard to move, to sit up, because of the pain from the surgery. Breastfeeding was harder; he never stopped. He grew and grew and I just got weaker and weaker. I went to a Bumps and Babies group but the women were not very nice. "You'll put that weight back on," one of them said, though I hadn't brought it up. "As soon as he's on solids and you start eating what he's eating. You'll put that weight back on." I couldn't care less about the weight, but I just nodded, and left soon after, gripping the handle as strongly as I possibly could, feeling completely invisible to everyone except my son, as anything but a body, a vessel, a thing.

———

The day before Valentine's Day, we decided to go to see a big ship that had been docked at the edge of the Tay for a hundred years. The previous night, as usual, I had barely slept. The baby slept for an hour and then woke up for a feed; stayed awake for another hour, content only to rest on my chest. Then, if I was lucky, he would fall asleep again, only to wake up again an hour later. In the day, he slept after regular feeds and long walks; life felt luxuriously intimate and desperate all at once. I was mostly alone.

I took the baby on more long walks every day and sat in a warm café, and talked more to friendly strangers and waitresses than my own family or friends. I was given advice about eczema from the man in the grocery store, encouragement from people sitting nearby or making coffee. I was not in my old life anymore; no one was familiar. And yet, this baby — new, but so familiar, so close. And this city. It was cold but I liked it.

The dislocation, emotional and social, confused me nonetheless. There was all this love, but everything was so different. My boyfriend was constant, in a way, but began to seem like someone in the distance. He was not there in the daytimes usually, as he was at work, and he was working on another new project while I nursed the baby, in the evenings.

When we went to the ship, which was called the *Discovery*, and had sailed around Antarctica, these feelings suddenly came together. The ship was not moving, and yet I had seasickness. The room swirled, the spot of ground I was on seemed to shake beneath me. I sat down. The baby was asleep. And the world fell in. I gripped the black seat and tried to fixate on the educational posters around me, telling stories of adventures and discoveries a long time ago. Brave souls, braver than me.

I closed my eyes. I tried to let the thoughts I had been repressing, the expansive loneliness, just wash over rather than drown me. I tried to reason these newer thoughts away — *I want to die. I want to die. I want to die.* I tried to focus instead on the waves, as if I was already there. *I don't want that,* I knew beneath the words, I didn't want that at all. I was in free fall, in this moment; thinking of death was a way of consoling myself that it couldn't last forever. Pain doesn't ever last forever.

Was I in labour again? It felt similar — this paralysing duel — this impossible, relentless, swelling pain. I didn't really want to die, but it was all my mind could spit out, the only way I could articulate it. Unbearable, all of it.

I wanted out, to not have to feel the pain, when there was no reason to. I was not in labour. There was no point to this at all. This wasn't going anywhere. It was just destroying me. The fear had turned into something darker yet, it had turned into the temptation of surrender.

The guilt at feeling this pointless pain, when I had been so blissfully happy so much of the time, drove me forward, though. I gripped the handles of the pram, and I got up. I was shaking but I steadied myself. It didn't make sense. It was just something I could push through, and bear, like I had done so before.

It was so cold outside, and the wind hit my face and I just kept focusing on that instead. How cold it was, how surprisingly harsh the weather could still be, after all these years.

It was just weather, though. Just a mood of the sky, in a cold season, on a motionless boat that had sailed the world and now sat here, entertaining its visitors with the stories of its past. What it has lived through, the men who had trodden on it. The ship could do it. I could do it.

We left the Discovery, about twenty minutes after, and I had something to eat, and felt better for it. I kept focusing on the cold wind, so as to distract from the other sensations.

Later, I could barely remember anything about the ship. Only the sea sickness, the vertigo, the trials you can go through on a vessel that has docked.

I was given questions about Post-Natal Depression, like all new mothers are, soon after this point, because I was at the point when a lot of new mothers experience a hormonal dip and develop it. I was just borderline, they said. "I'm better than a few days ago," I replied, and they nodded. "Tell us if that changes," they said, and I nodded back.

After that, I didn't get worse, at least not initially. I didn't have another moment quite like that, where the world fell in. I was so afraid of it happening again that I put everything into stopping it. I was mixed up, though. How could I be so blissfully happy and feel such a sense of belonging and contentedness, and yet be so on edge in these other moments? How could one day contain such contradictions? How could simply continuing to be and do what I loved so much be so hard? How could the person next to me, who was supposed to love me, have so little idea about any of it? How could he not look me in the eye? Was he even there?

People say that if you feel this way, you should just reach out and get help and talk to people, but there was no one there. No one wanted to babysit or hear that the birth had been difficult, much less give advice on the consequential flashbacks, shock and crushing moods. When it came to health visitors or doctors, I couldn't put it into words. It didn't quite match up with the questionnaires. I knew, in the end, it was up to me.

I'm so lucky to be a mother, I thought, after that, and looked at my son's face (he was the one person who really looked back) — at the soft brown hair and fingers grasping at my clothes and face. This thought, this little, perfect, growing person, grounded me and consoled me. In so many moments, I was more blissfully happy than I had ever been in my life. I had a purpose and a responsibility. I had love. It would be nice to have had more everyday support and people around and hours to sleep. Help with things like changing nappies and doing laundry and cleaning and care.

But did I really need that? No. Every day was proof that it was possible to do what at times felt impossible, to transcend feelings and sheer exhaustion that seemed, in moments, interminable. Every day, things got better. Even if I felt alone in this gradual ascent. Even though, on some level, I accepted this harrowing isolation once and for all and simply got on with it. I still had my son, after all. I had remnants of myself, too. We kept going. He kept growing.

As the weeks and months went on, and my son and therefore I slept more, and the days got longer, the blissful moments extended and the difficulties lessened. I healed from the surgery; scars faded and organs reorganised themselves. Why did I ever doubt this body and mind? They could recover, even as they nourished another little person — perhaps because they had to. Recovery was built in. I needed to untangle the fleeting from the endless, the love from the mere intentions of it, the wilted petals from the new buds. That was all.

—

When he was sleeping, I started drawing him. Very quickly, in case he woke again. His little lips, the way he pouted in his sleep, I wanted that on the page, I wanted his little nose, upturned. I wanted to remember the exact ways his strands of hair fell over his forehead, curled around his ears. How he stretched his arms to either side of him, up in the air, as if parachuting. I wanted to remember in a way drawing could record, but photography couldn't. His line, my eye, the line on the page. Pure, how he lay there. It saved me then and it saved me now. Drawing. Looking. The connection. Disassociation was cured by this line, this one simple act. I drew myself back to life. How could I ever forget?

Paper Dolls

When my son was still a baby, I found the diaries and notebooks my father had left behind. One of them contained notes for a novel he had wanted to write about his parents. "A wartime accident", the death certificate had read. People had doubted how accidental it was, but he had not. He had written, in his notes, that "*she watched as the sun dropped over London with a whiskey soda and then, much later, took her medication.*" He had written a version of her death in which she had not abandoned him intentionally. For all anyone knew, it could have been true.

But he didn't mention that the medication had been codeine, that it was just after her fifth wedding anniversary on a cold night in December. There had been a song by the Mills Brothers playing at number one for a few weeks before called "Paper Doll", about a man who wants to have a paper doll instead of a real-life girlfriend, because he has been so hurt that his own girl, Sue, had cheated on him. He'd rather have a paper doll, the song goes, so no one else can steal her. But he didn't write down this detail (and probably never knew), although, very briefly, he did mention the Polish officer she had had an affair with, whose whole family had been killed by the Nazis and who had travelled through Europe and the Middle East before reaching London and meeting her. He never hinted that she might have been pregnant with his child, though.

His father — her husband — who had been an officer,

returned to London to find his wife had died. Not from a bomb but from pills. He had been shot in the lung but kept smoking. He had been heartbroken but remarried. He died in his seventies of lung cancer in the remaining lung.

In his notes for the novel, my father imagined the Polish officer meeting his own father, in a hospital in Italy, and his father forgiving him. "Admission and confession", he had noted down, in the plan. And then: "Forgiveness and friendship". It's what I wanted for him too. It's what I think he was able to forge in art, and so, in a way, in life too. I took his, and their lives, as a sort of blueprint for my own recovery. The birth had traumatised me; it had brought back dark feelings and experiences, and now they lingered when I only wanted them gone. In some attempt to change the images in my mind's eye, I drew new things, new people — anything but the specific images that haunted me in the crushing, darker moments.

—

Although I had taken photographs of the flowers at my father's funeral, it took four years until I could face them again. I had buried them beneath so many baby photos that I had to really search them out, during a particularly morbid phase, after my boyfriend was gone for good, and it was just my son and I. I was in mourning for that relationship and my father all at once. I was confused by my own repression of the overwhelming joy and stress of new motherhood, swirling alongside these deaths — and suddenly, I wanted proof. Of what, I wasn't sure. Of everything I had briefly forgotten? I was in shock, I think, and I wanted to start putting the pieces together — photo by photo and drawing by drawing, until

I could make sense of the past few years. A death, a baby, a marriage, a divorce. All in three years.

When I found the pictures, they disappointed me. Or they just saddened me, in a way that was not consoling or meaningful. I wasn't sure what I was feeling or had wanted to feel, how pictures might change that. I was disappointed I was still sad and numb. But also, that these photographs were not representative. Nothing I had felt then was contained in these images. These shiny snapshots of funeral flowers seemed cheap and garish, compared to everything they symbolised.

I wasn't done with the process, I realised. I wanted to do something with my hands, as if I were touching them again, as if they were real. I was not done, even if, or because, these photographs were underwhelming. So I drew them, then — the lilies, roses, and their leaves. But even when I had finished new drawings, I still felt that I hadn't handled them enough, that I couldn't quite let them go.

I joined a print studio after that, and learnt to expose their lines onto nylon so that I could press ink through their shapes, create repetitions. I printed them in black ink, pressing them into damp sheets of paper and drying them, hanging on strings like freshly washed laundry. Everything was new again and again and again. It was strangely, comfortingly, relentless.

I hung them up to dry and then laid them carefully in a pile. It was as if I had dried them from the funeral. I wish I had done that, in a way. It would have been better. But the process, again — I found it therapeutic, I suppose. I was not looking for authenticity; that was the point. I was looking to create the same image again and again and again, to lose myself in the repetition, to doubt what even happened, to reveal the strangeness of it all. Doubting that it even happens, doubting he had gone ... Why was it still so hard to believe? I gathered the prints of flowers into a black portfolio and clipped them into place. I took off my apron and put my things away, then went home.

As the images stacked up, there were fleeting moments of catharsis; at other times the project seemed like an endless excavation, each picture another relic from the past that I had hoped would come together to give some grander explanation for the poison I felt persisted, but which did not. There was always another thing, a piece of shattered bone or a discarded treasure that was precious until I had retrieved it, but then became a mere remnant of something ultimately impossible to reconstruct, something I could not even give a name to.

How could I exist through this ever-changing sense of embodiment and disembodiment, where other people and events seemed so easily to take and dominate and disappear and turn away? How could I reconcile myself to life, and to the pain of loving and losing others? By drawing, I hoped to find a way to reappear despite everything, to be visible to myself again. I wanted to articulate and visualise the pain of losing others, and how I existed with and through them, as they did through me. But what good was this, really? I had been here before, I had traced my traumas. I kept doing it, but to what end?

I sat amongst these sheets of flowers. Flowers that had died long ago, just as my father had, as they all had, but which now lay flat and two-dimensional on the floor. Confetti, in a way, except whole stems, bouquets. This funeral parlour. But there was something there that I was still, somehow, not reaching. Some disease I felt a need to root out. A ghost of a cancer? A root of a feeling? Here were just flowers. Repetitions of flowers.

I had been using art as a coping strategy, but in a way it was only compartmentalising these problems and memories, enabling me to detach myself from the memories rather than genuinely healing the grief or trauma. I was repeating and repeating, so that they would become changed and eventually meaningless. They became something else. The original images had gone because I had repeated them to death.

Nan Goldin took photographs in Berlin and New York in the 1980s, the same time as Mapplethorpe, of herself and her friends at their most vulnerable and most intimate. In *The Ballad of Sexual Dependency* (1986), capturing the LBGTQ community as the AIDS epidemic tore through it and recording her own fraught relationships, her work might seem to epitomise the famous observation by Susan Sontag that "all photographs are *memento mori*". In these images of couples clinging to one another, or brooding apart, in bruised, heartbroken faces, and despondent figures, a sense of life slipping away pervades the otherwise casual but intense scenes. A melancholy attaches itself to figures in heavy shadows and make-up, the curves of figures and hair and embraces.

Photographs, in a general sense, can remind us of our own impending doom, our shared fate of death. We cannot escape this, even though the instinct, taking photos, is often the opposite. We take photographs to hang onto life, to linger in moments — to stop time. But photographs also record a moment that has already gone — a version of ourselves or others that has already, in some sense, died. The disappeared, though, seems to reappear. It is a magic trick, and a compulsive one. To see a likeness of the dead or the past, in our present time, in our hands: what could be more irresistible, and more dangerous?

> *"My desire is to preserve the sense of people's lives,"* Nan Goldin once said, *"to endow them with the strength and beauty I see in them. I want the people in my pictures to stare back."*[44]

But also:

> *"I used to think that I could never lose anyone if I photographed them enough. In fact, my pictures show me how much I've lost."*[45]

---

44   Nan Goldin, *The Ballad of Sexual Dependency*, 1986. Aperture; Revised ed. edition, 2012.

45   Ibid.

An engagement with photography, whether that of others or our own, and whether professional, artistic, casual or amateur, is an exercise in confronting loss. It is a practise that entertains illusion and reality together. It promises both the potential delusion that the dead still live and the heavy articulation that that which we hold in our hands or view on a screen is an image from the past which will never truly exist again, but in this alchemical form. Photographs facilitate fantasy and imagination. They allow our demons to take shape, our hauntings to fill paper and screens. They give us a way to idolise those we love, or might have loved. We can project all of our desires and fears, whether conscious or not, onto an image, a thing.

That a photograph records a time already gone doesn't mean we cannot actively engage with it, or that that engagement is futile simply because it is part illusory. We are conversing with gone things and gone times, lost people. My grandmother had gone, but she left photographs, an image of herself. And so I can converse and collaborate with her, in some sense, even though it depends on my own imagination and a suspension of disbelief.

Photography is alchemy. It is a trick of the light, captured. It pushes the limits of reality, allowing us to time travel, if only for snap shots, flickers of time. This is a dance with death; we are communing with spirits. At its most essential, it is simply a way of communicating — not only with the spectres of the past, but with the very alive and present people whose attention we wish to hold now, whose emotions and camaraderie we wish to engage. How better to communicate the raw emotion of grief than to show another person a picture of one departed, with the simple context that you loved them?

Photography holds the potential to be such a direct and

efficient means of communication, perhaps all the more stunning for it being, these days, also so casual and everyday. We are bombarded with images, and yet we cherish only a few. We invest them with so much meaning. While we can take photographs in order to compartmentalise and order the past or present, it is also an act of intimacy, an offering of empathy.

> *"For me it is not a detachment to take a picture."* Nan Goldin also said. *"It's a way of touching somebody — it's a caress... I think that you can actually give people access to their own soul."*[46]

Robert Mapplethorpe also embraced this empathic, spiritual side of photography. Though so many of his photographs give the impression of detachment, morbidity and numbness, his unapologetic confrontation with death, sex and the self gave his audience the language to confront these experiences in their own lives. In his still lives and his portraits of friends, all poised and exquisite in black and white, he gives these objects, bodies and lives a kind of transcendence, mimicking the tropes of the Catholic faith he grew up in and re-appropriating them into his own aesthetic spirituality. In his self-portraits, where he seems to stare down his own camera — and in the later stages of his struggle with AIDS, his imminent death — he is triumphant in the reality, fashioned with the tricks of light and time, that he has immortalised himself in the best way he can.

When lives have been erased, the effort to immortalise or bring back to life, even if only in a symbolic, part-illusory sense, is fraught. In W.G. Sebald's work, his grainy photographs offset the written stories and pilgrimages; they are evidence

---

46   Ibid.

of lives and places that have decayed or been lost, but in the context of the writing, they are imbued with significance, not in spite of their potential inadequacy as reproductions, but precisely because of it. These images are so clearly *memento mori*; they are the treasures of a long excavation, revealing, in their reprinting, so much that can never be found.

We process loss through this strange, eerie dance — between uncovering and imagining, reprinting and repurposing, filling in the gaps of time with technical flourishes — always aware, despite our nostalgia, that every reproduction is a mark of a new life, not an old one.

Sometimes I still visit my grief, these flowers. Perhaps I did it for the action itself, though — to connect my body, my hands and eyes, with the lost one, to hold something in my hands, have proof he was here. Other times, I think that it is only myself I am persuading still exists. And though it is morbid, I feel most content when I am tracing the line of another living thing, or a dying one — reaching out through these detachments and last grasps for one shared moment, crystallised, then gone. What I have feared all along is gradually eclipsed by the love that remains.

We typically shy away from processing and confronting death in Western societies, and yet how we ritualise and aestheticise death, and what this means for us all on an existential level, is so important and necessary. Though we are often bombarded with spectacles of violence, and we are aware of pervasive fear and anxiety relating to our own death and that of others (and often provoked by those spectacles, as already discussed), we tend to fetishise and detach from the threat itself, and our rituals remain jarring and removed. There is a sort of desensitisation that can happen, where we are surrounded by symbols of death and our own fear of it, but we do not fully confront and understand it.

And yet, whether through the sort of memorialisation and rituals, or through therapy or philosophy or just talking to one another, it is important to slow down enough to sit with the threat and certainty of death, as it is, and to understand that this certainty, or at least our reconciling to that fact, rather than endlessly running from it or fighting it, is the key to personal freedom. Heidegger talked about living authentically in this sense, and that confronting death is not morbid, but liberating. Only when we truly confront the fact of our eventual end do we truly realise how much we have now, how much freedom is ours already and how much meaning it is within our responsibility to give ourselves.

—

About a year later, I found photo albums that had once belonged to my grandmother, Susan, and began a project, and obsession, that would form the beginning of my healing of the loss of my father, and how her death had impacted him and, by extension, myself, and my own relationship ending. I began printmaking, using these photographs that seemed to reveal to me a person, my grandmother, I had never known anything about.

I would go to the print studio while my son was at nursery. I was living alone, and a single mother at this point, so my time was very limited and money was tight, so I worked fast. As soon as I arrived, I felt immediately at ease in the routine and relieved to be back — in this studio where everything was in its place and set up. In the screen printing area, tubs of ink were lined up on the shelves, stacked against the wall. Crimson, cerulean, ochre, peach, steely grey, blue-ish grey, a shining, sluggish black. There were cardboard tubs of transparency sheets on the sill, clear but smeared with the residue of old inks — black, grey, dark blue, partially scratched off, flaking. There were large sinks, where inks diluted and settled in puddles before being washed down the drain. Rags dyed a hundred different colours, lying out to dry on the side. Buckets, sponges, squeegees, plates, cleaned and drying out on the porcelain rack. I got everything ready: the ink, the screen, the tub of water, the paper cut the right size. The photocopied photograph for reference.

The original had been taken during my grandparents' honeymoon in the Alps in January 1939, as they stood together on the top of a mountain. Susan was wearing a leopard-print coat, her thick curly hair cut above her shoulders, looking very serious; Patrick was bending forward, with his skis, smiling. I wanted to give them colour, make her coat pop out as it once would have done.

I looked down at the nylon stretched over the wooden frame, taped around the edges so that there was a window the size that the image would be. I tried to imagine it there — the finished picture — one layer at a time. First faces and hands, then her coat, then the green mountains, then the sky. I imagined bringing them to life, these people I never knew — my grandparents — but who surely could explain so much. I thought of these processes like a spell, one ingredient at a time, one chant repeated over and over, in a ritual of resurrection.

I scooped some of the pink ink onto the bottom of the screen. I took the squeegee, drew it up, over the screen. Pressed it down, the ink passing through the nylon, clean and perfect on the paper beneath. Another, and another. Sheets of pink, some more perfect than others, some not perfect at all. I lay them out on the drying rack, twelve squares of pale, warm pink, drying flesh and shadow and sky. As the sheets dried, I cleaned the screen, the pink diluting with water and bubbling at the edges, the rags picking up the inky puddles. I dried the nylon with a hairdryer; it warmed in clouds, shrinking smaller as I held it up.

The faces dried on the rack, in rows, melting into the texture of the paper. I tried to see her, to imagine her, but I couldn't. She was somewhere beneath the ink, trying to emerge in each layer. She was something I was not sure ever quite existed, not as I thought of her now, anyway. But I let this one dry, ready to excavate a person through a delicate film of paint, in a disappeared face, caught once and then buried.

I missed him. This wound opened up, somewhere beneath my chest, and gnawed away at me in moments like this. Grief was imminent and diffuse. It didn't matter if I fed it or starved it of thoughts, if I acknowledged the pain or not. Silently, it nestled into every part of me, crying out for my submission, implanting itself in every fibre of my being. But I could not do it. I could not surrender to the pain, too scared of it. Nevertheless, details prodded at my armour, teasing my sadness out in snapshots and fragments — sometimes manifesting in physical ailments, other times in coincidences, triggering memories I could not shake.

He had seemed to exist in objects at first — a jacket, a scarf, a book. But these things lost their magic and then he existed just in my imagination, in things that had happened but which I could no longer quite grasp. Trips to the beach where he had handed out sandwiches and flasks. Berating the dog or cat for nothing at all. Foul moods. A charming smile. A person who never spoke, just smiled, or usually did not.

After that, months later, he existed in photographs, even though there were so few. I wanted to know what he was like before he was sick, before I was born, when he was young.

And then I found these one morning at home — the hidden photographs of his mother. Here were the good times, his treasures, the mother he never really knew. At twenty-one years old, before the war: trips to Caithness and Stirlingshire, their life together in Edinburgh. Her life before that, briefly, in London.

I wanted to know more and more, more than I could ever know. And so I began this thing, this project, of trying to reveal secrets in old prints but printing them afresh, by giving them new colours and scales, by doing it myself. It is as if, by reprinting them, and changing them slightly, I was working on a collaboration with her, even though we never met and there were now eighty years between us.

Why was I really doing this, though? I pushed the thought away as I continued my artistic compartmentalisation — that this was something else. Someone else. I took another sheet of paper and laid it beneath the screen and I pressed the ink through again, another sheet of flesh, so similar to my own. And yet so invented, so fresh and new. A rebirth, of a kind.

She was an old photograph, a person who had given me hair, eyes, skin… Perhaps also a tendency towards low moods, sadness, self-sabotage… for how much of that was genetic? I looked at her and honestly I didn't see myself — she looked more like my sister — but I knew that expression, that feeling. I tried to build her, and build myself, to block out all the other faces. The Old Masters: all these artists, fathers, exes, demons. On and off and off again. I thought of them too often, I knew that. I had been too easily won over, mastered, controlled. These demons I had invited in, or invited back, who had colonised my thoughts.

I imagined her, instead, as the paint slid over the nylon, as her image collected in these layers before me: her dark curls, crimson lips, her skis. I imagined her cutting her hair, organising a wedding, laying out outfits for the honeymoon. The leopard-print coat, the trouser suit — here they were now, glistening and wet in their new form, their new ink. What a perfect look. How I wanted to slip into her clothes, perhaps even her life, just for a moment — anything to be out of this present one, or at least the anxiety and loss that weighed it down.

Gradually, in this process of printing and transforming and repeating, I came to realise that I had wanted to bring her to life, in a way, to calm the inherited fearfulness that had been contagious, had been transmitted from her to my father to me. That I could never get rid of, no matter how far away from home, or him, I went. I had never been able to escape it, and it had started, in many ways, with her, and with her erasure. I had never known her, and never would, but by repeating her image so many times, as my father had watched a similar figure to hers in the cinema — at this distance, I could confront her existence and her legacy, in a way I could manage.

Both of us had, in our ways, sought to find comfort and catharsis in films and art, finding in an aesthetic distance the means to begin to come to terms not simply with our own traumas and fearfulness, but those of our parents. His detachment was rooted in her death; my fear was partly that I would continue this poisonous legacy, and somehow turn into her. I printed out her pictures by hand, repetitively and compulsively, to create a distance between our fates, whilst acknowledging our similarities, and some sort of love and connection, even though we had never met.

I wanted to reform the distorted stories that had been passed down to me, to open up and expose the true chaos and passion and tragedy of her death, which had been covered up out of shame and sexism and regret and fear. I wanted to set her ghost free and so set myself free by forging this new connection, by humanising her as much as I could. Art was better than *ressentiment*, better than disassociation and numbness (though they would often coexist). I was trying to find a way back to myself, through her. As I worked, I realised I had become detached from myself many years ago.

When I thought of fear now, I thought of distance. I thought of running away, and becoming detached, in fragmenting and separating and being separated — not only from others but from myself. I thought of the ways in which fear is operationalised, in political spheres, to distance people from one another, to turn people into distant objects and half-there characters, only suffering far away. I thought of losing myself, a cord between the mind and the body being cut and broken, and the terror that emanated from this brutal detachment — the trauma and tragedy of dehumanisation as a response to fear itself. The fear, it was here again, and it was a product, I saw now, of several heart-breaking losses, all entwined.

But one in particular began to stand out more, as if I had isolated a single layer in a screen print, as if only now I could see it clearly. That particular trauma, that event, that single break of the self into a million pieces, through the impulsive violence of another person. That, I saw more clearly than ever, now, it was that I had to revisit — realising as I did so that I had been turning and running away from it for a decade. It had been eroding me from within, all that time, and now I would erode it back, smother it in sand, my turbulence a crashing wave, a song drowning it out, once and for all.

The Art of Exorcism

For a long time, whenever I had a bath, I would have flashbacks to a morning in London when I was nineteen. Though it was warm now, it had been cold then. The hot water in the flat I was in hadn't been working properly, but I was so desperate to be clean that I filled a bath anyway. It was cold, an icy November morning, and I was already so numb I could barely feel that the water was freezing. I lay there still, safe. I had just run away from a house on the outskirts of the city, having been taken there in the middle of the night and raped. I was numb, but in the bath, also safe and contained. No one could get me there.

It was bright that morning but the curtains were half drawn. Looking up at the ceiling, then down at my body, white and distant under the freezing water, as if I had drowned, as if we were not in the same worlds anymore, my body and mind. Some connection had been lost, a phone line cut between the mental and the physical, the real and the confused. Disassociation — it looked like fragments of lightened dust around me, shadows in water, the warmth in a grey shadow. The distance between them, which had once been one.

It was at once comforting and disorientating, this chasm. There were now two choices: to stay and drown or to leave. Get out of the bath, keep running. Live in an in-between world, never quite there, here, one. My body was a crime scene without any answers. I was something to clean away, that could not be cleaned away. Something that bureaucracy and politeness would ultimately bury instead.

I looked for others to complete me after that. I fit badly with the matching voids of strangers. I looked for intimacy in shared wounds, in scars that join each other, sort of. That's what had brought me here again. Another man, another bath. I closed my eyes, felt safe and numb and here again, repeating myself, my ritual. Poisoned, cleansing water, a still pond.

Over the years, this ritual of cleansing and disassociation became somewhat healing; the flashback became contained and transformed and I learnt to sit with it, to sit with my own terror and to let it (literally) wash over me. It was a place I could come back to alone whenever I needed to. In some ways, this experience was similar to the ways in which I used printmaking to process the legacy of my grandmother's suicide for my father, and his death more recently. It reminded me of Freud's writing on the "Compulsion to Repeat" whereby, through repeating once traumatic experiences, people transform their relationship to those original experiences and so diminish the power that the root traumatic memory has on them. While masochistic behaviours could work in a similar manner, a behaviour did not have to be masochistic to function this way.

Other repeated behaviours probably were, in hindsight, quite masochistic. I wanted to reclaim my body, which for so long felt like it was no longer mine, and for a long time, in some attempt to do so, I sought others to dominate me, so that this ghost would not dominate me. Satisfaction was only ever fleeting though, and healing powers of this approach somewhat limited. It took a long time to realise I had to dominate myself, to free myself; I had to step back into my own life and body and mind, and not desire simply others to do so. Escapism led nowhere, in the end, and other people, it turned out, were simply a form of that. I had to take my own power back — an idea that seemed alien to me at first, and almost irritating as well. It seemed like a superficial affirmation I could not really connect with or fully understand. For many years I did not want my power back; all I wanted was escape.

But lately, I had started to confront what I had been turning off, out of necessity. I had developed a phobia of the tube, shortly after my relationship fell apart — and in particular the Piccadilly Line. This was how this fear manifested now, along with a fear of being alone. I sympathised with people who were scared of public transport after terrorist attacks; in a way, in this small personal way, I was going through something similar.

Since arriving back in London, now a single mother, I had taken various journeys, mainly to see old friends who I'd lost touch with since university. I wanted to see as many of them as I could to reconnect myself, and yet I underestimated how much I hated the tube. I wasn't sure why — why I struggled to breathe, became panicky, even looking at the long blue line. Half the time I ended up taking a sedative just to help me breathe. To calm the agitation and claustrophobia those carriages inspired, with their rough fabric seats in primary colours and geometric patterns. Uncomfortable, anonymous strangers, dirt smeared like ash against the windows. A clogging scent that always took me back to a particular journey. I was so used to repressing it all that it took me weeks to realise that the tube was taking me back there every time I used it.

It was almost ten years ago now, when I had finally found my voice and told someone what had happened, here on the Piccadilly Line, going into central London — how I needed help. But the man — about thirty or so — looked at me blankly, first, and then with a vague sense of derision. "You should be more careful then," he said, and then promptly left.

After the rape, I had taken the train back to Scotland for three months and stayed the entire time in bed. No substantial food but occasional toast, no drink but tea, until January, when gin replaced tea. Of all the drinks, gin? Not a good idea. Memories refused to be drowned. There was no room for me in the house, so I was living in a wooden outbuilding, which had originally been built as a studio or office but which now had a bed in it. When it had first been built, a couple of years ago, I moved in willingly and happily, because it was the first time I had been allowed my own space — a bedroom of sorts. It was not, however, the ideal place to live in the middle of winter. Though there was heating, there was no bathroom or kitchen, so I would have to traipse in and out of the main house if I wanted to have a shower or make tea. At this point, however, these inconveniences barely registered. I lay in bed with the same numbness as that first early morning — the jarring, delirious silence — anaesthetised from what still seemed an impossible reality.

Hours passed and I didn't move. I had been cut off from myself. My own body seemed like a shell, something left over, something that used to be mine but was now detached, gone. I pulled the duvet around me — I closed my eyes, and I started to cry. It was now a week after it had happened, and the first time I let myself accept that it was true and irreversible.

I had woken up numb with shock, but the crying brought me back, although to a reality I do not want to be in. I didn't want it to be true, but I knew then that it was, that my memory was not lying, just pushing pieces of me through to the present.

When some of the shock subsided, and I started crying, I started drinking gin instead of tea. I stayed with the gin for the next few months, then years. I would live in pieces, otherwise. A part of me — one of those pieces — wished that those fragments had been left in the past — left at that moment of breaking — left and let go of. I did not really know how to live anymore — how to live in fragments. Pieces jarred — desires jarred — my entire sense of self had become a sense of perpetual conflict — a consistent not fitting together. I could hardly hold myself — this new self — together.

But from the moment I first admitted what had happened, I also realised a whole expanse of moving upwards, through some Underworld, at once mine and not mine, a perpetual fearfulness. I cried because it seemed impossible. I knew that pretending it hadn't happened was no longer an option; I knew that more and more remembering, and retreating, and remembering, and running, and then remembering, was the only way I could be. I knew I had been sentenced to an impossible, shifting, punishment — or challenge, in more optimistic moments — that I was not prepared to deal with. I was nineteen. I didn't feel prepared for anything.

After the initial shock wore off, I slipped almost automatically into various ways of escaping this sentence. Although it took months before I felt like eating anything again, I started drinking as soon as I had to start living again. As soon as I had to see people, and go out, I started drinking. I may have sometimes drank before, mainly because everybody else was — but now it was a drug, that I consciously let myself depend on. It was never strong enough, but it was something to hold on to.

I couldn't be myself again, but I could be drunk. And that seemed a little more socially acceptable, and therefore viable, than being some sort of faint ghost, some pale dead thing. I did not want to be lost again, but since that seemed to define every waking moment now — this being lost — I drank to forget I was lost. At the time, it felt like it was saving my life.

I went back to London in the spring. I went to all the festivals and met vampish men, who swayed tall and smiled and then got arrested. I did everything possible to blank out everything and everyone except the music, and the dry green grass, and those others sharing their bright despair, casually.

I kept dancing to forget — shunning the lonely, crashing moments, those memories that seeped back into consciousness in the early morning or as I walked down empty streets, haunted. I kept trying to forget, but I couldn't help thinking about it every day — every hour — in between the songs and new people and the romance of summer. They followed me everywhere, these bullets of memory skimming around my head. the Fear. It crept with me, usurped me. I kept fighting it, and yet I always fell back. It had never fully left; my life had felt like an endless journey through the Underworld. It was so familiar I just became accustomed to it, as if it were part of my personality, rather than an affliction or a learned response, or a protracted haunting. And yet, sometimes, like now, it would re-emerge more forcefully, and though my mind found ways around it — excuses, rationalisations — my body began to resist the intellectualization which masked a form of denial, a sort of escapism.

In the underground again, I tried to shake off this feeling, the growing phobia of the train, and the tube. But it continued with each journey. At least on an above-ground train, there were views to distract myself with, a sense of real escape and movement. But on the tube there was just dirt and claustrophobia, clinging. And yet, I had not connected the anxiety, the phobia, with the trauma. Even after all these years.

Instead, I was at a loss: Valium didn't work so well anymore. Maybe I just had a bad dust allergy? Not anxiety, after all. Maybe I had got it wrong. London was very dusty, the tube, especially, was very dusty. Perhaps the trigger was actually physiological, and environmental.

And yet, *the Piccadilly Line*. It was always worse there. Was I allergic to a particular dust particle on the Piccadilly Line? Or a memory? Was there all that much difference? I took antihistamines, felt a bit better. But still, my heart raced. If I hadn't been physically ill before, I was now.

A few days later, on my way back from an exhibition, I took the Piccadilly Line again. I was heading North West, and the train stopped at Acton Town. It was busy and noisy, so no one could really hear what the conductor was saying. One person said that the train was continuing, while others got off. I asked one of the other commuters: "This is going north, isn't it?"

"No I think it's going to Heathrow, now."

"Oh no!"

The other passenger laughed and then I tried to laugh it off, too. I got off, had a sit down. I tried to breathe normally, but could not. It was not just dust, then. As I sat there, I imagined how bad it would have been to have ended up in that direction without realising it, if I had somehow ended back in Feltham. That familiar dread, that nausea. Every Piccadilly Line train I'd been on. I hadn't really connected the two things before, though it seemed obvious now.

I kept looking at the tube map on the wall of the train, at the stops and area I had always avoided. I was tired of being scared. I had sedatives in my pocket, but I was sick of needing them. I remembered Paris, and how, in the end, my fear of my father's death, which had become inescapable and crushing, was only assuaged by going to see him again, by going home, and so facing my fears. Perhaps now, too, I realised, I would need to truly confront what I was scared of, or remain terrorised by the Piccadilly Line indefinitely.

—

I used to imagine going back to Feltham. It had started with the police. When they had driven me around the various identical looking streets, to see if I could remember anything more. I couldn't, which disappointed them.

I wasn't sure if it was some deep-seated desire to please them, but I began to imagine what would have happened if I had, in fact, remembered something. If I had recognised the man himself — how would the police have reacted? If I had said, "that's it! That's the house!" — would they have driven slowly past, again and again?

In some ways I was relieved, at the time, that I didn't recognise any house or person in particular. I didn't know how I would have reacted, but I doubted it would have been in a relieved or satisfied way. I imagined I would have been terrified.

Nevertheless, after the journey around Feltham had ended, after I had gone home, I wondered how things might have been. And then, in the privacy of my own imagination, I went back alone. I roamed the streets I only vaguely knew; I looked out for faces, passing.

I imagined if I had seen his wife and son walking down one of the streets, sometimes — would they be smiling, like in the photograph I had noticed in the hall, on my way out? Or would they be looking sullen, like I imagined they must really be, to have to live with that man. I couldn't have been the only one, I found myself thinking. Perhaps he did it to her, too.

I remembered her long, curly black hair, bright eyes and a pretty smile. A handsome son with cropped dark hair, only a couple years or so younger than me. Maybe they were not unhappy at all.

When I imagined going back to the house, various times, I wondered what I would do when I was there. Would he be alone? If his family were there, then what would I say to them? Would I tell them what had happened, or die trying? I didn't usually dwell much on this scenario: I skipped ahead to the version of this story where he was at home alone.

I imagined that I would have taken something suitably dangerous and violent with me — a knife, perhaps? I wasn't a fan of spilling blood, even if it wasn't my own, less still actually stabbing someone, so I thought about alternatives. A baseball bat? Too cartoonish, really (though practical enough). A gun? A little hard to acquire, probably, and this scenario had to retain some semblance of realism. I would trail off at this point, in my dream, and just settle for a knife, even though I knew I would prefer not to use it.

As the scenario played on, I realised that I didn't actually want to kill him, anyway. It turned out that I just wanted to look around his house, initially — the room and hallway I remembered, and then the ones I didn't see. I didn't know why I wanted to do this, particularly.

After I had meditated on these details and taken a long look at the ordinary looking double bed that now had such significance for me, I would go downstairs again. I would open the living room door, and I would watch him. I imagined that he was watching TV, in an armchair, oblivious to me. His face was lit up by the moving images, starkly. He was probably eating something.

I wanted to know who he was. I wanted to just wait and watch, as if that would tell me something I didn't know, as if it would explain things to me, as if by observing this man, I would understand why he attacked me.

———

I went back there on a Monday, around lunchtime, when my son was with his father. It was a crisp and sunny day, and after I dropped him off I was tempted to go to a park or a café, rather than go on this depressing pilgrimage. It seemed a good day to have lunch with a friend, perhaps, rather than to retrace the setting of a personal trauma. And yet I had committed to the plan; I was determined to see it through.

"*If you see something, say something,*" a billboard read, as I took the escalators down, after a short bus trip. I went through to the platform for the Piccadilly Line going west and sat on a bench. As I waited, I looked at the tube map again, at the various stops:

Gloucester Road Earl's Court Barons Court Hammersmith Acton Town South Ealing Northfields Boston Manor Osterley Hounslow East Hounslow Central Hounslow West Hatton Cross

I tried not to think about why I was going. The man next to me was listening to music, a tinny drum beat audible and irritating, but at least breaking the silence. Grey dappled tiles on the floor. Signs: WAY OUT. *I could still leave,* I thought, and yet I stayed where I was.

A man with a suitcase sat on the remaining seat. I exhaled, hearing the train shuttling towards us. How many times I had thought about jumping in front of it. And how many times someone else had jumped in front of the train, and everyone on board had complained about it. *So inconvenient, so selfish,* someone would always say, as others merely sighed. *If you're going to top yourself,* I once heard someone say on a busy train, *then why not just take an overdose?*

I got on the train, where someone's perfume dominated the carriage. It was warm and sweet and not especially seasonal; it was a heady rush of late Spring — tones of hayfever — not this icy winter's day. I sat down on one of the purple and blue and grey seats, and briefly glanced around — there were so many suitcases, because people were going to Heathrow. Others were reading papers and looking at their phones, avoiding one another. A man with a guitar got off at Gloucester Road, and it reminded me of nights at the Troubadour when I had lived nearby, that strange, jarring time of glamour and dirt, in awful things seeming romantic on account of someone good-looking singing about them in a certain way.

As the train moved overground, the sun poured in. There was so much dust on the windows that it was a film of white. I saw chimney pots, rows of terraced houses and bare trees. Suitcases and Christmas shopping. A church spire, office buildings.

At South Ealing I became uneasy, perhaps because the train had passed the fork in the tracks where I could go in another direction. My stomach turned and my chest ached. Whenever the train stopped I worried we were stuck.

Northfields Boston Manor

There were shadows and sun flickering in the windows: serious, absent faces. One man was talking constantly about a renovation: "He has to put a valve in there, freeze it... If you've left that turned off, how am I meant to get there? Idiot... There's no shuttle valve underneath." A park, trees.

I started getting cramps. I looked out at the blue skies. I

closed my eyes and pretended to sleep. I was already tired of looking.

As we got closer, I kept getting surges of adrenaline, reminding me I had committed now, I had to go.

At *Hounslow East,* I took a deep breath. I had come to this or the next station to see the police. I felt so alert that I was shaking; it hurt, as if my skin had suddenly become more sensitive. I tried to focus on other things. Cranes, terraced houses, a sinking feeling. Tiredness began to accompany the alertness. *Hounslow Central.* I tried not to think about it. *Such a bright day.* Light streaming in.

I got off at Hatton Cross, heart fluttery, on edge.

I walked out and saw the H26 bus to Feltham Young Offenders Institute waiting outside the station, and I got on. I could see the airport to the left, and BA signs everywhere. I looked at the bus driver — was it him? No.

He smiled at me. His features were sharper.

The bus left the station and I looked out of the window — it was all just construction and cars. Metal fences, car parks, a smell of fast food and sweetness. Some raggedy ponies in an overgrown field. And then, quicker than expected, we were there — the houses I couldn't tell apart.

The first street did look familiar. I looked at the bus stop sign: Cains Lane. We drove on. The next stop was Hazelmere Close. It could have been one of those too. A police car was parked badly on the pavement.

West Road. A child got on with his mother: "See ya later," he said to a friend, "Love you." The next stop: *Horsham Road.* It could have been that one. But most likely, we had passed it now.

As the bus drove on again, I realised I'd been blaming myself for not recognising the house, but now it was clear that I couldn't have. These streets did look the same. I'd narrowed it down to a few, which I recognised even now, and I had told the police as much as I knew. I had tried my best. It was not my fault they couldn't find him. Not my fault he had disappeared in plain sight.

I relaxed for the rest of the trip, understanding why it had been unresolved for me. Knowing the bus had probably passed it, now.

I sat back, and watched the surroundings more passively, thinking that I must have watched these things go by as well. We passed a cemetery, and some trees being planted in rows and green plastic casing.

And then we were at Feltham Young Offenders' Institute. There were logs in rows and mud to the left of the car park. There was a park in the distance. I remembered this loop very clearly, and it was a relief, strangely, to see it, as if it were an old school I had left. At the bus stop, there was a sign about getting home using cabs and minicabs. A lady in her fifties got off. I read the sign about the prison:

"The best chance for offenders to turn their life around."

There was something funny about that. In a way, I identified with it.

I had felt that I had been given a long sentence of punishment following the attack, starting ten years ago, when I had first been on this bus, and first driven past this prison. Now, in seeing it again, it felt as if that sentence was finally being lifted. As if I were leaving finally.

The bus drove off, and I began to wonder how long it would take to get back to the station. I remembered that the bus went around in a loop, so it would go back eventually, but I couldn't remember how long it took.

It took over an hour, it turned out. As I'd passed Feltham prison at least four times, before, and each journey passed it twice, it meant I must have been on the bus at least two hours originally, possibly three. I was surprised I didn't have more of a phobia of buses, from this experience.

We went past more bus stops. If I didn't have a phobia before, I was getting one now. *Get a life, bin that knife,* another sign read. It was starting to become difficult to take anything seriously now, with all these symbolic statements everywhere. I looked at my watch and wondered what time I'd be back in London. I saw planes landing at Heathrow.

Eventually, the bus turned into the tube station, and I got off. As I left, I felt such a sense of freedom and elation. I had done it. I'd gone back, and I'd found out why I'd been feeling this lingering stress, why I always felt like a failure for not recognising the house. I could forgive myself now — of course I wouldn't have been able to tell them apart. It was suburbia.

I had to forgive myself for being scared, for being in pain, for being the victim of someone else's violence. I had to stop blaming myself for something I did not do. I had to remove myself from those around me who had blamed me and shamed me, and offered no support or compassion. I had to find my own self-worth, and heal from the neglect and cruelty I had experienced when I was younger. I had to make my own home, find my own sort of love, my own sort of freedom, and grow in that.

Like an old injury, trauma causes fresh pain in waves, often unexpectedly. But I don't feel lost or ashamed anymore, I don't feel worthless anymore. People do care. There is always so much to be afraid of, but knowing people care begins to heal the trauma that accentuates the Fear.

As I travelled back, I felt a sense of relief, that I had confronted my fears, as it were. But the relief was accompanied by a sense of anti-climax. What now? So I had gone past my rapist's house on the bus I had taken to escape it. Did he even live there now? It didn't matter. That's what I couldn't help but think, now. It didn't matter. It didn't matter who he was or where he was; "he" was one more vague ghost and only I really remained, now. And for whatever reason, I felt alone, isolated, drawn away from the world.

I felt annoyed with myself, then. Why did I keep being drawn back into a past I had no place in? Why did these memories live in me, make me sick, when I had so much to be happy about? Why could I not just let it all go?

The trip took another thirty minutes, on the tube. I sat there, numb and tired. I had to compose myself, again, for my son this time. And wasn't I lucky? Wasn't life so much better now? Couldn't I just be happy about that?

I emerged from the Underground, at South Kensington. I texted to check where they were. They were at a café a minute away, and I went there. We sat down. Here I was, chasing old demons, tracking them down. Why had everything entangled like this?

"We went to see the dinosaurs!" My son said, joyfully. He was happy, fine, eating a cookie. I hadn't needed to worry.

"Me too," I mumbled, and then gave him a hug.

"Mummy snuggle," he said, burying his head into my chest.

Yes, here he was, here it was. I had a new life, now, a new focus and love: and he was perfect. It was blindingly sunny and we had seen the dinosaurs who no longer actually posed a threat, and we were going home. "I'd better be off", his father said, and said goodbye. My son climbed onto my knee and finished his cookie.

We went back to my friends Charlie and Janina's house after that. At first they were away, but later they came back, and I told Charlie where I had been, the morbid pilgrimage I had been on. He knew, too, that the divorce had just come through. He looked at me in a kind way and we didn't need to talk about it anymore than that.

When the baby was asleep, Charlie poured us glasses of champagne, sitting at the kitchen table. His warm, glowing, face. Usually irreverent, but beneath that almost serious now. There had been so much, over the years. There was something perfect though that it always ended here, or at least paused here: Charlie pouring champagne, candles, stars, a smile. There was that, whatever weird journeys we departed on and came back from.

—

The next night, Janina built a bonfire in the garden and they threw a party. She had made a Yule Goat from straw for a design job, and, according to Swedish tradition, we wrote down all our problems on pieces of paper and burned them to cleanse ourselves. "It used to be that people would write down their sins and put them in the straw," Charlie said, "but we're just doing general problems". I wrote down some names, the men in my life, and one in particular — a nameless name, but a name all the same. I watched it burn, alongside everyone else's problems. We all had them, and now they were all in flames.

Having very recently finished my thesis on demonisation and scapegoating, I found it funny that I was watching a literal scapegoat burn on a bonfire, with a bunch of people standing around as their problems were symbolically absolved. Clearly this was a much better form of "scapegoating" than capital punishment, either televised or the historical versions that I had studied. And yet, I could see why a (non-violent) ritual like this was important. I certainly felt better for it, realising in a basic sense that I was not alone in being haunted by people, by having problems, by wanting them to go away. It was relaxing, to see the straw burn problems into a vast, prickling light, and then disappear them, if only for a moment.

We went inside and had drinks and dinner, and the destruction itself was not important; the symbolic, communal element was. Before, I had only ever been alone with my thoughts and my traumas. For a few minutes, I had been surrounded with others, and though they didn't know the details (they didn't need to), I became one with the crowd, the burden divided up.

Rituals are important. The need for catharsis and community is especially so, but there are better ways of processing fear and death than what we as a society currently seem to engage in. When religion, whether pagan or Christian or Muslim or Judaism, is less prominent (and even when it is not), society still finds ways to perform these rituals, to process death and tragedy and terror. Some are simply more violent and cruel than others. The Enlightenment was never more present or persuasive than Romanticism; it simply won the debate for a time, tied to the logic of colonialism and empire and patriarchy. But we are emotional creatures, acting accordingly and inescapably. To be aware of that is key to reconciling with the emotional and soul life that society is so keen to compartmentalise, commercialise, pathologise and exploit.

—

Exorcism is an art — from horror films to cathartic art practices, and from TV shows about falling anti-heroes to superstitions and religious rituals, people find many creative ways to relieve themselves of the terrors and fearfulness that linger in their lives, whether related to specific traumas or more diffuse threats or worries.

When I took a journey to Feltham, it was in hindsight quite a dramatic, intense way to try to exorcise that demon and to face my fears.

In many ways it did help, though not quite as I'd expected. In truth, I did not know what to expect, only that I wanted to face it, to somehow cut the cycle of flashbacks and claustrophobia. What happened in the end was that I realised I needed to forgive myself for not remembering where the house had been. I hadn't realised it, but I had blamed myself for the police never finding anyone. I'm sure, too, that I had also internalised all the shame that was put on me by people I told at the time, which took all those years to begin to shed.

This is perhaps one reason why fear interests me in the ways I have outlined so far — no matter how much we turn it over in our minds, often the origins of persistent fearfulness are things we do not specifically remember or give attention to. I assumed it was the attack itself that was continuing to traumatise me, but in a way it was actually other people's reactions too. It was the lack of help from that man on the tube, it was the reactions I got when I went home, the lack of privacy, and the incessant, eventually pointless calls from a detective who could not solve it either. It was not knowing, and not solving, and not getting any answers. It was having to deal with it all alone, and to deal with a massive sense of betrayal from those closest at the same time.

I think this is why these journeys and rituals can be useful, just as normal psychotherapy can be too. We can find out things about ourselves and the environments we were in that we would otherwise overlook. We can therefore find ways to cut the cycles of fear and shame and self-punishment — to see the reality of trauma more clearly — and then finally move on.

—

After this personal exorcism, with the tube journey and the Yule Goat, after the screen-printing and then some painting, after writing, after a divorce, gradually I began to turn back towards myself and the physical and future world. I stayed in Scotland and started writing art reviews as well as teaching, while my son started nursery.

I went to an exhibition called *HOLE* by Glasgow-based artist Margaret Salmon, which was inspired by the work of bell hooks and which I was reviewing for a magazine, shortly after I got back to Scotland from London.

The exhibition began with a literal hole in the wall that the artist had punched through herself. Visitors had to walk through this hole, this person-shaped void — rubble still everywhere — to get into this overly warm, dark gallery, where different short films were shown, with a recording of writing by bell hooks overplayed on a loop: *"Love and abuse cannot co-exist".*[47]

I heard it and then repeated it to myself. It played over and

---

47   bell hooks, *All About Love: New Visions (Love Song to the Nation)*, William Morrow, 2016.

over. It seemed so wise and yet so impossible. It was something I couldn't fully grasp or believe.

It was a quote from the book *All About Love*, in which bell hooks dismantles notions of love predominantly defined by romantic desire, and shares a vision of love that can be ethical, communal, equal and healing. The exhibition was a celebration of this apparently superior sort of love — real love untainted by power imbalance and patriarchy.

The exhibition included a collection of films, showing couples intimately together. True intimacy: this was what it is supposed to be about. Sex that was truly, lovingly intimate. So why did it make me feel so depressed? Why could I not write about it?

Even now, I couldn't work my way out of it. I just kept watching the films, these couples together, and how depressed it all made me feel. Was I supposed to write that? That other people being happy together just opened a wound in myself? Of course it did. It reminded me of what I didn't have anymore, of what I had perhaps never quite had — this hole in myself.

Hands touching and becoming entwined, before disentangling — a palm brushing against a face tenderly. But they were on these monitors that looked like CCTV monitors; I was forced to be the voyeur, watching these strangers and the love they had and the love I didn't have.

I went around the corner and then there were more films — more couples having sex, as passages from *all about love* are spoken. "*Love and abuse cannot co-exist,*" the voice said again, as two women embraced. This was the new romantic ideal that despite myself was lost on me. I was not in it; that was all I knew. I didn't have whatever this was. I had lost it; he had gone. I kept looking at the hole in the wall.

What had I been doing all my life? Was that not love too?

Surely it was? I couldn't accept that it wasn't. And yet, it was not this. It was not what bell hooks said was love. I could not deny that.

Later on, when I was back home and my son was in bed, I looked at a blank page on a computer screen, imagined the artist hammering through it with a chisel, emerging darkness on the page. *HOLE,* I wrote down. I kept writing, as if my words were her chisel, opening up these rooms of reflection and destruction, the gaping spaces in which to congregate. This hole, this wound, this missing thing. I could not just sit with it, I had to make it even bigger, I had to smash more of the wall in myself. I had to own and love my fury. My fury was part of my strength, an expression of hope.

Facing fear can become an obsession, a loop, an inescapable circuit. It can become behaviours that distract and sabotage recovery and healing rather than promote it. Healing can feel desperately elusive and difficult without guidance and vision. When I visited *HOLE*, I felt bereft; the void, the wound, was there right in front of me, and it hurt. But eventually I started writing about it, and simply acknowledging the hole in me, the aching wound, the haunting traumas, and it set me on a path to recovery.

I started reading bell hooks and then Audre Lorde. I stopped running from my own fury, my own anguish and my own demands. I realised, even if I could not fully stop, the masochistic cycles I was in. I started to envision for myself, one day, a world in which love was beyond this loop, because, as bell hooks said, as I had heard repeated to me in the gallery, "love and abuse cannot co-exist".

I thought about Nietzsche again, about his idea of moving beyond both slave and master mentalities, or at least evolving them. I remembered how I had read that Nietzsche considered

Jesus Christ to be a "proto-*Übermensch*", forging new ideas and ways of living, independent and subversive. I kept thinking of forgiveness and self-mastery and the connection between them. Of grace as strength. Of forgiveness of oneself. Bringing power and energy back to oneself. Radical self-love. I thought of Audre Lorde, and her collection of essays, with its perfect title, *The Master's Tools Will Never Dismantle the Master's House*.[48]

I thought of the past and its legacies. The need to forgive my ancestors for their legacies in me, and trying to correct them in the present, the need to forgive my family, where I could. Forgive careless and cruel and narcissistic men — and women. Forgive myself for feeling pain, and feeling alone, and not wanting to live. Forgive myself, and them, for being human, for being weak, for repressing the strength and beauty that were always possible.

The only real antidote to dehumanisation is humanisation and grace. Sometimes that may require forgiveness. Sometimes it may require ritualistic activities that gradually replace one dehumanisation with a new understanding or pattern of behaviour, or relationship to pain and the past. Sometimes it requires art and poetry and singing and dancing. Always, it requires faith.

We find our own ways. We eventually find ourselves and then one another. We find that the world does not have to be a terrifying place, at least not all the time. We find we can start over and over again, burning straw goats behind us.

It is difficult to admit our own weakness, and these rituals and art forms (for what is art if not ritualistic) are ways of bridging those numbing, lonely distances, the chasms between

---

48   Audre Lorde, *The Master's Tools Will Never Dismantle the Master's House*,
        Penguin Classics, 2018.

people and within ourselves. They are ways of admitting our own humanity and the frailty inherent in our nature. It took a long time to accept my own vulnerability, and to allow myself space — from others, from pressures, from shame. I had internalised the fearfulness and powerlessness of another person by force. It had been internalised, I should say. I did not choose it.

But years later, I realise I have choices. I must accept my own vulnerability, but also my strength. I am not only a woman, for instance, or a victim, or a passive thing, even if these roles and states characterise some aspects of my lived experience. It has given me immense insight into the behaviour of other people, and especially men, to be put in a position of victimhood. I may have been treated as an object in the past, but I have never actually been *just* an object. I have seen everything. There is a sly and enduring strength in my own perspective.

That is why we are considered a threat, I think: we can see what they are doing. We bear witness to their greatest crimes and their deepest failures. We can see them in their moment of weakness. We can see right through the façade of strength and into the depths of human frailty.

For some people, to be seen in this way — as all of these things — is actually a relief. It is to be seen as a human, however damaged and damaging, and not just a man, for instance. Perhaps at the root of so much violence there is also this sad, confused desire to be "real", however brutal that person may be. Repressed emotion, repressed fear and shame and anger, come out in these ways, hurting innocent people, and destroying their reality for the sake of another's ego. But over time I have come only to pity this weakness, to see that brutality and egotism is a cry for help, an expression of absolute weakness masquerading as strength, the deepest need for validation through the physical disintegration of another.

For a long time, I did not understand the point of forgiveness, or really the meaning of it, but I think now that I understand this, I do. For all the bravado and violence of men and women, the worst of them are only human, merely deflecting from the vast void at their core.

Kunst und Angst
(We Are All Mad Here)

I found it hard being a single mother, with no regular help with childcare for a long time, and living in Scotland, just the two of us. Despite all my intentions and convictions, and the real blissfulness of motherhood, which I loved more than anything else — how fun and sweet and beautiful my son was — nevertheless I struggled. I was always sleep-deprived, and because it was just me at home with my son, it meant I was house-bound most of the time. Every evening, as soon as he had gone to sleep, I couldn't leave our flat even to buy some milk, or go for a walk, because it was illegal, of course, to leave him, and there was no one else to mind him. So while I enjoyed our days together, which were always sweet and fun and busy, with this beautiful little boy — in the evenings I was entirely alone and trapped.

As the months and years of this went on, the aloneness transformed into crushing loneliness, a severe feeling of claustrophobia. I also started to worry, since it was always just us, about what would happen if I got seriously sick or injured, what if no one could find us in time? I would have bouts of panic where I would imagine that if I collapsed or anything like that, my son would be completely indefensible — unable to phone anyone, or call for anyone, unable to open the front door and ask for help. It felt impossible, and impractical — cruel, really — for us to be so alone and isolated and for so long.

As these concerns piled up, I began to feel eclipsed again by something bigger than me, and greater than all my good intentions. I struggled more with insomnia and anxiety, and then I found it hard to eat enough. I had no time to myself at all, when the nursery holidays started, and so I could no longer go to the print studio or have time to work properly; it was harder to meet anyone, and also to pay bills. And so I found myself sinking. Art had saved me, and having work to do had given me a sense of structure; but when there was no more time to draw and print and write, I fell apart like a plant lacking water. I couldn't meet anyone for a coffee, let alone a drink; I couldn't go on dates and I barely saw friends.

A resignation came down over me, around the time of my birthday, and a new wave of depression began to consume me. It felt that this time, it wasn't going away, that it was threatening me on a different level, in a worse way, somehow. That this time, I couldn't go back. Something had to change, I kept telling myself, and yet I couldn't see what. What exactly did I have any control over? What could I really change? I had tried everything now. A part of me didn't care, and yet I couldn't function either. I was despondent and strung out, every physical movement painful, too much.

I cut up apples for a morning toddler snack, put cereal in a little bowl, filled his cup, and hated myself for being so empty of life in these moments, a robotic, tired thing, when he was so perfect and so sweet and so full of energy. My love for him broke me sometimes, after a night of not sleeping properly, made me weak and confused. He danced and thrashed around, wanting more attention than I could give. The guilt of my own weakness destroyed me further.

That night, I fell deeper into it, whatever it was, this inky, endless thing. After a few hours, I talked on the phone to someone at the end of a helpline, something I never thought I'd do. I wanted any voice, any voice at all, to distract from my own internal one, increasingly a phone off the hook, a gone thing, confused.

Hello, this is Christine.
— Hi. This is a helpline, isn't it?
Yes.
[Pause]
Our remit is suicide prevention.

— Oh good.

Is this the first time you've phoned us?

— Yes.

Well let me tell you a bit about who we are. We're set up for suicide prevention. Everything you say is confidential. However, if you are worried that you may not be safe from yourself, or someone else may not be, then we have a team of advisors, and if we think you're in danger then we can phone the emergency services.

— OK. Well I'm not about to kill myself. But I am thinking about it a lot, and I'm just getting really sick of it. I've had it before, and I get through it, but I'm just really tired of it now. I thought I've moved beyond it but every time I think it's in the past, it comes back again. And this time it just feels really sudden, and really bad. I keep doing everything I can to stop it but it doesn't work.

Like what?

— Well I've got medication to take. I've got lorazepam for times like this, and zopiclone for insomnia. But this time nothing has worked. I still can't sleep and nothing really touches it. I can't eat or do anything. I have no energy. And it just came on.

Is there anything you think has triggered it?

— Well yeah. I'm exhausted. I have a four year old and he's been acting out a lot lately. I got divorced recently. I was seeing someone and they broke up with me. I never see my friends. I've been trying to get a better job for a year, because teaching and writing doesn't pay enough, but I barely have time to do the applications. I'm just really, really tired.

Well that is a lot to go through. And it's very recent. So it's not surprising really.

— I just worry that it's always going to be like this. I'm always going to end up back here. And I feel so guilty, with my son,

for being like this. Imagining ways I might go. I don't want him to be alone like I am. I don't want to disappoint him.
You don't need to feel guilty. This happens to a lot of people.
— I feel like I'm stuck in this personality that gets thrown down by these things and I wish I was different.
But this doesn't define you. It's not you.
— Maybe.
Have you felt like this before?
— Yes, lots of times. Since I was a teenager. I kept thinking it was because of one thing or another but now I'm not sure. Maybe it's just me.
How have you kept going?
— There are things that help. Creative things. Writing, although now I think maybe it makes it worse, because I dwell on things more. Painting. Just seeing friends, walking around. Guilt. Not wanting to be like my grandmother. Wanting to get better. Wanting to be different. Wanting to be here for him, always.
It sounds as if you've become good at finding coping mechanisms over the years, ways of pushing forward.
— Yes. But now I just feel like it's too much. I used to always assume that I could get better and I was optimistic. I thought there was some solution to the problem. But now I don't think there is. I made an appointment with a therapist, though. I'm going to get more childcare for my son, to stop myself getting so exhausted. I think, in a way, I've been trying too hard to do everything by myself. But I can't anymore. I'm not invincible. I might not get better. I have this constant sickness, stuck in my throat at all times, to remind me that I wanted to kill myself two days ago.
If you do feel that way again, you can always call us. If you don't feel safe from yourself.

—

When I was eighteen, I went to Vienna. It was not the first time. My godparents lived there, and were from there, and I would go and stay with them in the summer time. It was a home away from home. We would spend time by the lakes and then go to museums in the city, look at paintings and masks and clowns. I had always enjoyed myself, but this summer, I did not. I loved it there but something stopped it getting through to me.

I kept getting lost in the parks and streets and having panic attacks. Not sleeping. Trying to compensate for being terrified by acting fearless. Trying to turn it all into stories instead — using writing to transform this reality that was fractured into something that made sense. Wanting to have a substance abuse problem so that I was not just crazy. I did not tell people I was delirious from sleep deprivation and fear. I started writing novels instead. I read philosophy and became good at turning disorder into order, or at least arguing that I had done. The delirium stopped, then. I thought I had found the key. I suppose I had found one key.

I came back to Vienna again a few years later, when I was twenty-one. By this point I was a terrible insomniac again and a chain-smoker. I drank too much and took too many drugs. My relationships were a source of deep misery. Even I knew that these were not really the problem, but they were something to do, something else to talk about. An articulation of heartbreak, which was very real, but inescapable, because no one else had really caused the underlying problem, not entirely anyway. Everything was entangled and complicated, even then. I didn't feel myself, but it was OK. I was in Vienna. My godparents' family were writers, therapists, artists. They probably knew I was struggling, because at times, everyone did. It was not taboo there, but it was still terrifying. But I was safe. The people were kind. Egon Schiele looked down from the museum walls; he knew, too.

The next time I returned to Vienna, I was twenty-six and six months pregnant. I wasn't unhappy then; I was probably the most harmonious I had ever been. The baby bump was just about showing, and he was kicking, softly. I had everything to look forward to. I had cravings for dumplings and schnitzel and sips of beer. Apfelstrudel. Roses and paintings. It was the best time. I was safe again. I belonged, somehow.

I needed to go back now, I realised. I was at the point where I didn't feel I could look after anyone anymore. It was hard to look after myself. To eat anything, to think about basic things.

I remembered being like this before, in Vienna, being so paralysed by tiredness that I didn't leave the apartment I was staying in for three weeks. The idea of the subway or a map terrified me. Occasionally, I went to a small shop on the same street for minimal items of food, but I struggled to eat, and then I struggled to sleep.

Why had I been ignoring this pattern for so long? I had been noticing all of the others. I had seen the connections in every other area. But the whole time I had been playing down what now seemed the one consistent thing. These lows, these crashing lows, even if I had managed to pull myself back. The anxiety and the paralysis. The panic attacks. Illness, which weaved its way around everything else I loved and hated in life. It came on suddenly and then it left swiftly, but how could I forget it? The Fear — it was this, and it was back. It was a void greater than I ever remembered.

I thought back to labour, and I thought back to my father. I knew and had known for a long time that that was my way of coping; to play it down, like he did. To get through each time, and then to move on, almost forgetting it had even happened. To convince other people I was fine, and so convince myself too.

—

After asking my ex to look after our son for a few days, I booked flights to Vienna, using money I'd been given for my birthday from my friend and mother-in-law. "You deserve some time off," she said. "Have a wonderful time there." I wanted it to be a holiday but it felt more like I was going to a sanatorium, trying to get my head back together. Exhaustion was an understatement. I had been sleep-deprived for three and a half years; I had not slept through the night once in that entire time.

"I love you," I told him. "I'll be back in four days. It isn't very long, you know, and you'll have a nice time… I'll bring something back for you." But even packing seemed a struggle — remembering basic things to pack, booking a hotel.

Everything seemed impossible. I scrolled through a bookings website and could barely focus. Was it better to stay here? Just stay in my room for a few days, uninterrupted? But I needed to go, needed to be somewhere completely different. There was something about Vienna that promised an escape, a consolation, somewhere that I could hide in.

On the flight, I sat by the window and tried to relax, as the plane swayed from side to side. This quiet terror still held me though. As if I had changed, and I could not go back to who I was. The man next to me started up a conversation. He was in his early forties, wearing a light tan suit and an open shirt, sunglasses in his lap. "Do you live in Vienna?" he asked.

"No, just visiting. I've been a few times before though. My godparents live there."

"Oh that's nice," he said, with a light Austrian lilt. "It's very hot there at the moment, though. Most people will be out of the city."

"I know, but I don't mind. I have a couple friends who are still there, I think. I'm really just going for a bit of a break, anyway."

"I'm sure you'll have a nice time."

"Do you live there?" I asked.

"Yes. But I travel a lot for work. Frankfurt, Edinburgh, I'm always away. I take this flight every month."

"Are you staying long this time?"

"No — I have to be in Frankfurt again on Friday. I'll see my family though, which is nice."

The air hostess came by then, and we ordered coffees, and our conversation trailed off when I started listening to music with my headphones and he half-read a magazine, flicking through pages about other destinations.

The hotel I had booked myself into had a wine theme, and the mini bar was stocked with a selection of notable Austrian wines. My room was called the Riesling Suite. I lay down and just stayed there for an hour, eyes closed. Happy. This was how life had once been, sort of. At least in moments. This freedom. I was so unused to it now. I could never go anywhere freely anymore. I had tried not to dwell on it, but I really had missed it. I was anchored in this little person, our own family of two. I missed him now, as if a part of me were missing. But to lie here — eyes closed, skin relaxing in the heat that drifted in from the outside street, everything pristine and neat and spacious — I had missed that too.

An hour or so later, I went out for a walk. Even the buildings seemed to transmit heat and colour in yellow, ochre, peach. I walked past careful window displays of complex lights and chairs and chocolates. Flowers, a little wilted from the heat. Most of the shops were closed for the day. The man on the plane had been right — the city was quite empty — but it suited me. I walked and walked and walked, until I realised I was hungry. I hadn't been for days, weeks. I had been making myself eat small things to keep going. But now I was hungry.

I sat down at a bar, the closest to me, at a table outside. A waiter came over. "Just one?"

"Yes, just one." He laid down a menu and napkin and cutlery, left and then came back again a moment later. The other tables were full of small groups, laughing over beers.

I ordered schnitzel and some Austrian white wine he recommended. The sky turned a deep, bright blue, a blood moon, somewhere, casting its heady glow. I ate slowly, carefully, trying to taste the food that still seemed like paper in my mouth. The wine helped it down.

When I had finished eating, some boys sat down at the next table and I asked them for a cigarette; we got talking. They were skaters and musicians from somewhere in Germany, with their friends who were in a band that had played the night before. Soon more of their friends arrived, and I joined them for more drinks, as lightning lit the sky, weirdly unaccompanied by thunder or rain. We talked about where we came from, about psychology and politics and painting. At eleven I left, and walked back to the hotel, remembering previous times in Vienna with boys, and thinking that perhaps I had grown up and got better after all.

Back at the hotel, I ran a bath and drank some wine. As it got later though, I got sadder again. I felt like a shell, deflated and odd in my own skin. I had lost weight and hardly noticed before. The only reason I noticed at all was that people kept telling me I had. A health visitor had commented on it when she came to see the baby once. "I can tell your son's a happy, healthy wee boy," she said one afternoon. "I'm not worried about him. I'm worried about you. How have you been?"

"I'm tired a lot," I said.

"Are you eating?"

"Not much. I'm just never hungry. Food is tasteless, I just can't eat, even if I wanted to."

She asked me about depression and told me she had been a single mother too; she had left her husband after an abusive situation. Things got better, though, she said.

"You could try to get an appointment for counselling," she went on.

"I think the waiting list is about a year," I replied. "Maybe longer."

"It's better to be on the list, at least."

"OK."

"And you can always call me. Here's my number."

Maybe I should have called her, but here I was. I needed

to get away. To remind myself I could exist beyond Scotland, beyond that flat, especially, beyond it all. In the weird lighting of this new hotel bathroom, though, I stood there and barely recognised myself. I didn't like it, especially. I looked like one of those skinny Egon Schiele girls, gaunt and strange. Not myself, not quite myself.

I slipped into the large bath and lay there a long time. I had taken a Valium but that feeling seemed indistinguishable from what I usually felt. Memories still came, and with them, a tired restlessness to be rid of this. I remembered the baths before. This time, being given a bath during labour. It sounded nice but it was awful. The pain was unbearable, the bathroom clinical and claustrophobic. It was hard to get out in all the pain; I dribbled blood on the floor as I gripped the side, like my whole body was an open wound.

I distracted myself with some shampoo that smelled nice and a package of bath salts with a lengthy description about the healing forests that had somehow manufactured them. I closed my eyes and lay back and began to care less, think less about the other baths. I began to feel irritated instead. Why had it taken all this just to have a single break? Had I not been assertive enough? No, I had been. But nothing was ever enough. Being assertive enough was not enough. Had I not communicated myself clearly? Why should I have to?

I got out of the bath, anyway, face to face with my apparently emaciated figure, now. Perhaps in some subconscious way, that was a way of communicating. It was the only thing people ever commented on, the only thing that seemed to draw concern. You would think that everything else was obvious enough but being a little too thin was what people noticed, not objectively difficult domestic situations, or looking miserable. You had to physically be fading away to be seen.

I would try a different tack, though, just to see. I wanted my ex to know what I was going through, how it couldn't go on, how I needed help. I went and sat in bed and I wrote him an email.

> *I used to always have this determined spirit that would sort of rise up whenever I felt like this but now it doesn't. I keep falling back. It doesn't matter what I do anymore. It's like that point in labour where despite all the many hours of putting up with pain and dismissal, and then doing what I was told, and pushing and so on and doing everything I was meant to do, it still all just failed and I was wheeled into surgery. That's how it feels. Like I'm being cut open.*

He wrote back quickly: consoling and kind things. *You haven't failed,* he said — *I'll help more.* The recognition that there was a need. That I couldn't just always do everything myself, all the time, endlessly.

I put away my laptop and tried to sleep again, but I couldn't at first. Slowly though, the wine knocked me out. As I lay there, listening to people outside, I remembered the story I always told my son before bed. I had made it up one night and he kept asking for it. He called it *The Space Story.* It was always slightly different, but it also always went something like this:

> Once upon a time, there was a little boy, who lived with his mummy, who loved him very much. And he had a spaceship, parked in his garden, behind their house. At the end of the day, just before bed, even though he was very sleepy, he went to the spaceship, opened the

door, and went inside. *3, 2, 1, Blast off!* Up and up they went, up through the Earth's atmosphere and into space. Where shall he go tonight? *The Moon.* The moon. He went to the moon, parking on the edge of a crater. And when he opened the door, there were lots of funny little aliens, wearing silver, and dancing. And he went down and danced with them, until he was too tired to go on, and then he went back to his space ship. *3, 2, 1, Blast off!* He zoomed back to Earth, and back to Europe, and back to Scotland, and back to his mummy. And when he landed back in the garden, his mummy gave him a big hug, after all his adventures.

He would always respond with his own story. "And now, Mummy, a story about *you*... Once upon a time, there was a girl called Mummy..."

Remembering that, I fell asleep too.

———

In the morning I emailed a couple of friends to see if they were around. First I contacted Karin. I had first met her about ten years ago when she was going through a divorce. She was about my age then and had three young children. She had just decided she would retrain as a doctor, much to everyone's surprise. Everybody was telling her it was a ridiculous idea. The second time we met, about five years ago, when I was pregnant, she was training to be a psychiatrist. Now, she was a junior psychiatrist and psychotherapist. She was about to finally finish her training. "This is great timing!" she said on the phone. "I just got back from holiday. I hurt my ankle, actually, but I'll be fine by tomorrow. Breakfast? I will text you a place. 9am?"

"Perfect, that would be perfect. Thank you."

After that I emailed my friend Dylan, whom I had last seen about five years ago in Paris, the day my father died. He was now a philosophy lecturer at the university in Vienna, specialising in nostalgia and anxiety, and he and Audrey were married. We also arranged to meet the next day, near the Leopold Museum, for lunch.

The rest of that day, I had no plan and did not feel up for much, so I just went on walks — to parks, cafes and around in circles. It was very hot, but I liked it. I didn't think as much, or worry as much, although there was always a slight terror, caught in my throat. I bought some cigarettes, and smoked as I walked, or in a café, with a soda water. I went to a bookshop and browsed for a long time, feeling less isolated by doing so. *KUNST & ANGST* was one of the titles. I felt at home.

For dinner, I went to a little Turkish restaurant with a terrace and ate a starter. I still wasn't very hungry, but it tasted nice. As I walked back to the hotel, through quiet streets, I began to feel a pressure lifting. And yet I kept feeling the need to be careful, not to let this despondency swing another way, not to let myself be over-enthusiastic or just dismissive of how it all felt now. This time, however, it didn't really feel like an option. My mind was so foggy and tired; my whole body felt weak. I couldn't really imagine just bouncing back, like I had sometimes in the past. That didn't feel wholly negative though; despite how bad I felt, it seemed overdue.

On Sunday, I went to the Leopold Museum early so I could see exhibitions first. I went to see Klimt first — all of his women. Standing in black dresses, with their graceful melancholy, their bed hair and scowls. The rooms were darkened like vaults.

I sat on a bench and worshipped the male figure, the goddesses in red and gold. The cycle of love, life and death — bodies entwined and transcendent, together. The art gallery had the feeling of a church and I worshipped quietly.

> In *Schubert at the Piano (1896)*, for instance — an ethereal, otherworldly study of the pianist in profile, surrounded by girls and warm tones of red and cream — the beginnings of Klimt's development of a sensual, expressionist style are evident and absorbing. In *Friends (Sisters) (1907)*, painted nearly a decade later, Klimt presents a glamorous woman in a long black fur coat and velvet hat, with her sister behind her in similarly striking attire. The elongated and formidable figures, although in an everyday scene, create a sense of tension and admiration — alluring and enigmatic in their quiet, compelling drama.
>
> Eight years later (or a roomlater, in the exhibition), the famous *Death and Life (1915)* is a bold and defiant vision of humanity, in its perpetual dance with death. Creating a sort of waltz, its entwined lovers, mother and child, are especially luminous and mesmerising, displayed in a dimly lit room within a room, where the colourful figures shine out against the retreating, but ever-present melancholy of death.

After Klimt I went to see Schiele. I had last come here when I was pregnant, and had looked at the paintings of mothers and children, which were discomforting and yet weirdly consoling. Tense, natural embraces; black clothes. Angst at every single life stage. "Dead Mother": a haunting, dead-eyed woman, swirling around her baby, as if she were a dark sea he had been caught in. I wrote down notes, for the review I had said I would do:

> Schiele's self-assured subversion of traditional painting and his development as an expressive painter; the presence of "the mother" and children in his work (Dead Mother, c.1910, particularly beautiful, however melancholic); his interpretation of ideas related to religion, spirituality and individual transcendence; atmospheric houses and landscapes; and the highly charged interrogation of individuality in his self-portraits. The latter theme, presented as a room of "Egons", is particularly entertaining and even charming — for all the machismo and youthful angst, there is something quite tender about Schiele's readiness to bare himself in such a direct and fearless manner.

These stark faces, these bodies, unfurled. Here all these feelings and experiences were normal, simply because they were painted there. They took up room, these shades of angst and pain. Perhaps repression of these feelings was as detrimental as they were alone. Simply seeing them was consoling.

I spent more time in the room of self-portraits — with Schiele himself. His comical bravado and masculinity, his intensity and neurosis and more black clothes. I loved Egon, despite myself. I kept looking at him. That face. I kept looking and the more I looked, the less I saw the different men in my life and the more I saw myself. Had I been haunting myself? Had I been afraid of myself all along?

I thought of pools of red, of Narcissus and Echo, of Jean Cocteau and all the mirrors capturing our gradual deaths. Had I been evading my own reflection all along? Had I been chasing all these men in some misguided attempt to find myself? Here Egon was, standing unapologetically. Not ashamed, but bold. Here he was, in the art gallery, waiting for me. Here I was.

I read about Klimt and Schiele after that, and their friendship. Their love and respect for one another. Their entangled bodies, their dances with one another and the ideas they wrestled with. It was as if they were in a dance, a duet of sorts, some hypnotizing show. Vienna, a waltz. *The twisted, tortured figures seem balletic at times, even as they express passion and angst with every muscle, line and graceful, if pained, pose.*

Before I left, I sat on another bench, under the gaze of a female nude, wild and defiant and detached all at once. I remembered when I had been in the Musée D'Orsay, just over four years ago, when my father was dying, and saying a little prayer, or something vaguely like one — that he would know that I knew how hard he had fought, and that it was okay for him to stop, to let go. That it was OK. Perhaps I needed to tell myself the same thing. I needed to let go of the pressure to hold everything together, to not be sad. I didn't need to be afraid of it. It didn't mean losing my mind; it was the opposite of that.

After seeing the exhibitions, I waited outside the museum for a while, where I'd arranged to meet my friends Dylan and Audrey for lunch. I sat on a sand-coloured ledge in the bright noon sun, which was too bright even with sunglasses. I sat there anyway though, remembering what my friend had said about wanting to lie on a rock in the sun by the sea, barely leaving. I tried to settle into it, to submit to the sun, be more like that, and more like him. I got a text from Dylan, saying they would be ten minutes late, and took out a cigarette, lighting it as more languid tourists stepped by.

After a while, I saw Dylan and Audrey's familiar figures the other side of the square. Despite the life changes and time, they both looked exactly the same as four years ago. I went down to see them. Dylan was wearing all black clothes and black sunglasses; and Audrey was wearing a red floral top and black trousers, with a red scarf in her hair, like a Fifties pin-up. We took shelter in a nearby café and ordered breakfast. I asked them how they were. "We're all good," Dylan said, smiling at Audrey as he said this. "Audrey is pregnant, actually."

"Oh that's wonderful, congratulations," I replied. They beamed. "How many months?"

"About five. We haven't really announced it to many people though."

"That's so exciting. Will you stay here for the birth, then?"

"Yes," Audrey said.

"We have a nice apartment," Dylan went on. "We're lucky. It's very spacious. Although there is the usual worry about short-term contracts, of course."

"I can imagine," I replied. "Every job I look at is a one-year contract, somewhere far away — it's difficult… But it will be fine. When they're babies, it's actually quite easy to travel around."

Our lunch arrived and we talked some more about Dylan's academic work and Audrey's translations. Then they asked me how I was.

"It hasn't been the easiest summer," I admitted. "But it's good to be back here. My mum's babysitting for a few days, so I took my chance to get away for a bit. I needed to have some space to think. I've been doing everything and it's been too much."

"That's hard," they said.

"It's nice to be here, though," I replied, not wanting to be too negative about everything. "I think I just needed a break."

After we finished eating, we walked around the square for a little while and I took a photograph of them in the sunshine, beautiful together, before we parted ways.

As I walked to the hotel, taking a long way back, I kept seeing babies with their parents, and in those moments remembered how sweet having a tiny baby had been. I missed that time together as a family, despite the flaws. In those early days, I could not have foreseen that we would end up apart.

Back in the hotel, I lay there, tired from the heat again. I took my phone and started looking through old photographs and drawings from when my son was a baby: this serene, beautiful boy, blinking in the snow, and then lying amidst daffodils when he was older in the spring. I put it away and then remembered more: images, flashes, screens that captured something that seemed so surreally gone, now.

My last day in Vienna, I met up with Karin. She was tall and blonde and smiling, glamorous in a dress with a tropical print, and tanned not only from the heatwave but from a holiday to Mauritius. She was limping slightly, from an ankle injury, but she smiled brightly. We met at the 25 Hours Bar, where a neon sign greeted me: WE ARE ALL MAD HERE, it said. *Willkommen.*

"Hi!" she said, so warmly, and gave me a hug. "Is this OK for you? I thought we could go inside. They have all the breakfast things there. We can sit by a window though."

I followed her in, where she seemed to already know the staff, or at least be so friendly that it seemed that way. It was a buffet system, and we took trays and loaded plates with an array of things. I had eggs and toast. "Are you sure that's enough? You can have anything you know. I am paying, of course." I smiled; she was so warm, maternal.

"This is great," I said.

As we ate, I told her about the past year and especially the past month. I told her about the divorce, about relationships since. I told her about the traumatic birth, the early days with the baby, so full of pain as well as love. Perhaps because I knew she was a therapist, and she encouraged me to talk, I felt comfortable talking to her about the insomnia and thoughts of suicide, the panic attacks.

"Did this get significantly worse after the birth?" she asked. I thought back to then. It had been on my mind of course.

"Yes," I replied. "There were moments. But I think it was circumstantial as much as chemical; I think it was because I had no help, no one in my family was there to help, and then there were all these physical problems after the birth, and then after that having to work full-time without childcare, and then the divorce... And he still wakes about three times every night. It has just all gone on a long time. And also, I think the birth itself, because it was traumatic, it made all these other past issues resurface. So I don't know whether it's post-natal depression or PTSD or a mixture of a lot of things, but it has been harder in the past few years."

"Of course," she said, refilling my coffee, "after everything you have been through. It is a normal reaction to trauma, to all of these things. Do you have anyone to talk to back in Scotland?"

"Not really, no. I mean I have friends. But professionally, no. There is a waiting list of over a year to see a therapist on the NHS, and it's too expensive privately."

We kept talking. She asked me about times before, about other behaviour. "I think you are a perfectionist personality," she said, "but you don't have to have it all together all the time. You don't have to be perfect. You don't have to struggle. There are good medications out there... Though I would stay off the barbiturates. You've had these periods of trauma-related depression, but have you had any — heightened — behaviour?"

"Not exactly," I said. "I've had insomnia since I was nine, though, and sleep deprivation can make you think you're losing your mind. And I have a tendency to overthink and overdo things, especially if I'm stressed. I think that writing was a way of containing that impulse sometimes. It gave me a way to focus my energies. It was a way of trying to figure it out, too, the patterns of behaviour and why I reacted as I did. But now, I don't think I can keep doing it. It isn't really working anymore. I'm just tired of everything. Relationships especially — I always get too involved. It doesn't matter what it's called or what I tell myself. I always get too involved and then I'm miserable when it ends. Like the whole world has ended."

"After my divorce," she said, "I promised myself that I would never let anyone hurt me that much ever again. You can keep your distance. You can make sure you're safe. And then, when you're truly ready, you can get involved. You can still have drama and love and everything — but you can be safe too."

She decided she would drive me to the hotel, where I would check out, and then we could have lunch somewhere. We did that, and went for a walk around the first quarter. We went into shops and she bought a little present for my son. We had a coffee with her husband, and a cigarette. Then he left and went back to work, and we had lunch in a beautiful little place with tropical plants and fruits and wicker chairs. "You must eat," she said. "You will get your appetite back, bit by bit. Here — try this." She spooned some dessert onto my plate.

"Thank you."

"Everything will take time," she went on. "There is time to figure it all out, and find the root causes, but right now, you have to act so that you are not in pain. Whether with medication or not. You need to detach, and let other people help. You need to delegate wherever possible. And just enjoy the small things." We looked around us — the trees, the flowers, Vienna.

"That's why I love drawing," I replied. "It's a way to just stretch out those moments, meditate on them."

She smiled. "Good."

Karin took me to the train station to go to the airport. I was shaky and sad, but I knew things would be OK. Not in a grand and glamorous way, not in an immediate way, not in an ecstatic way. I felt so terrible, so physically drained, but for whatever reason it seemed that this was healthy, normal, human. It was sickness but it was also resistance; my own body had gone on strike. No more, it said. My heart was tired, and it ached, and for once I listened to it. I sat in the airport bar, drinking an apple juice, waiting to go home.

—

School started at the end of the summer, and we enrolled in the primary school around the corner from our flat. In the weeks before, I collected little white polo shirts and grey trousers, fitted new school shoes and bought him a little maroon cap to match his jumper. He auditioned for drama school wearing a magician's outfit, sitting on a padded bench with the number

100 attached to his black t-shirt, a sparkling black cape around his shoulders.

On the subway back, he sat by himself, across from me, seeming nonchalant, but then smiling at me, proud of himself. He had got in. He would start singing, dancing and acting classes in a couple of weeks.

Each month, a new part of himself grew and flourished. Once he would never have strayed from holding my hand; now, at just four, he seemed so independent riding the Glasgow subway, peering around.

He was one of the youngest in his year, but also the tallest. He was very nervous on his first day, but held it together, holding a school bag with pirates all over it. For the first time in nearly five years, I had my days back to myself. Six hours each day. And yet of course I missed him.

But everything changed. I went to cafés to work, started job applications and more freelance work. Sometimes he came home for lunch, if he was feeling like it, but usually he stayed in school all day, and I picked him up at 3pm finding it so surreal that I was now a parent of a school-aged child. When he was a baby and toddler it never seemed surreal, but being a parent at the school gates did. *Parent/Guardian.* Surreal, but a promotion of sorts. When we walked back together, I was always so full of pride for him, as he held my hand again, tightly.

—

One week, soon after school began, I went into Edinburgh to see a new Paula Rego exhibition so that I could review it. I met my two friends, Sam and Miranda, and we had been standing in the first room of the show for about three minutes when an irate man interrupted us, eyes bulging. "Excuse me!"

he bellowed, a few inches from my face. "Will you please stop talking! I am TRYING to HEAR the PAINTINGS!" Sam burst out laughing, and then quickly corrected himself. "Oh," he said. "You're not joking." No, he was not; his aggression was entirely, unreasonably, intentional. A middle-aged man loudly trying to silence us.

We left that first room; as we walked towards the stairs, I warned a couple going in about the man we had left behind us. "Maybe I should start whistling!" one of them said. "Please do!" I replied.

We went upstairs to find Rego's *Dog Woman* series — works produced over the course of Rego's career, from the drawing *Dog Woman* (1952), made the year Rego entered the Slade School of Art, and met her partner, painter Vic Willing, to *Sleeper* (1994), one of her first pastel works, in which a woman lies on her master's jacket like a sleeping dog. Throughout these works, which marked not only different stages in her career, but also in her life and particularly her turbulent, complex relationship with Vic Willing, the central themes of obedience and defiance were clear and vindicating. They gave me fire, lit me up, elevated something that had been shy to come out.

Having grown up under the strict and oppressive fascist regime of António de Oliveira Salazar in Portugal, I read, in which the state and the Catholic Church worked complicitly to control their subjects (especially women), Rego's work consistently and defiantly addressed complex power dynamics in various intersecting areas, whether through the prism of personal, romantic relationships or through overtly political issues such as war and political exile. In her Dog Woman series, she used the image

*and mannerisms of dogs to explore the nuances and
complexities of these power dynamics.*

Sometimes a master, sometimes the obedient dog-like creature,
Rego's characters equated female and male sexualities and
other behaviours to the characteristics of dogs, and in their
associations with one another, and other overt motifs from
political discourse and Portuguese folklore, she connected
these seemingly distinct issues. Was the master her husband or
the Church? The king or her mother? Her own sexuality? Her
characters, regardless of their roles, dominated us all with the
same compelling combination of defiance and submission to
their roles, their physical (often constrained) form, their closed
and confusing environments.

We walked around some more, taking in the domineering
submissives and constrained masters: in *Snare* (1987), a girl
in a voluminous mauve dress loomed over a dog, mocking
its powerlessness and impotence. In *Untitled* (1986), another
young girl, wearing a hairband, put a chain around the dog's
neck. Later on, women themselves resembled dogs: in *Sleeper*
(1994), an adult women lay in a doglike pose; it was not clear
whether she has been punished or whether she takes comfort
in nuzzling with her master's jacket — or indeed, both. In *Lush*
(1994), another woman sat openly like a dog, moody and yet
unapologetic. In the *Abortion Triptych* (1998), women stoically
endured illegal abortions out of social and financial necessity.
In *The Crime of Father Amaro* Series, a young girl is caught up in
an illegal affair with a priest.

I sat down and read about Rego's life. She had met her husband
Vic Willing at the Slade when she was nineteen and he was
already married. She went on to terminate several pregnancies
as a student before going back to Portugal to have their daughter.

They later married, after he left his wife and they reunited, and had two more children. He then developed multiple sclerosis and Rego became his carer in the later years of his life. Their roles therefore evolved in complex, difficult ways: Rego was a young lover, a "fallen woman", a mother, a wife, a carer.

Life necessitated stark changes in role, far more complex than notions of "master" and "dog" would at first glance explain. But her paintings revealed precisely this: how binaries of power dynamics were simply markers that signalled vast depths of human emotion, as we struggled to love and endure one another in wider systems of oppression. I thought of them all, then. How we struggled to love and endure one another, on whatever level.

And then I couldn't help but forgive, though I had not been trying to. I never really intended to, wasn't sure I ever really understood the point of forgiveness. But I couldn't hold it all against them anymore. They were people in paintings, creatures, twisted and dark and sublime. I'd shared their shadows long enough to know that much.

> *Though she sought to be a painter, "like a man" —*
> *an "art monster" — Rego could never escape being a*
> *woman, just as her subjects could not (and perhaps would*
> *not) escape being dogs,* I wrote. *Their passion is wrought*
> *from sacrifice. In* Sit *(1994), a pregnant woman crosses*
> *her feet, and in so doing mimics, subtly, the Crucifixion. In*
> *the series of etchings exposing the horror of female genital*
> *mutilation, Rego's victims recall tortured Saints, despite*
> *the brevity and minimalism of their production. Using*
> *these familiar motifs from religious paintings, she elevates*
> *the everyday suffering of women, recognizing it and*

confronting it head on, never losing the nuance, ambiguity
and darkness implicit in these scenes and situations.

Rego saw the similarities between art practice and romantic relationships. "Painting is erotic," she said, "you do it with your hand. It's the same feeling of being possessed by desire". In painting, as in eroticism, she was defiant, even as she was consumed. All of her characters were defiant and consumed in their situation. All of her artworks were defiant and consuming. They depicted suffering, oppression and cruelty, and yet her figures consistently embraced it.

There was a film showing downstairs in the gallery, and we sat down to watch it. It had been made by her son and also featured her daughter, who said of her mother that endurance of pain became a sort of proof of love. "Look how much I will bear for you," her paintings seemed to say — and not simply to her late husband — but to life itself, and to God, despite the Church. "Look how much I must love you, to endure all this."

The film also talked about how Rego had suffered from prolonged periods of depression, and in those times she "draws herself out of it". She "gives fear a face", and in so doing she masters it. There was a sense that in these images of suffering, confused desire, love and pain, Rego mastered these forces and people in the act of painting or drawing itself. She endured and expressed aggression; she was the Master and the dog — to painting, to desire, to the political environments she found herself in, often viscerally.

I walked around some more, leaving Miranda and Sam by smaller paintings, and came across *Angel* (1998), part of *The Crime of Father Amaro* Series, in which Rego depicted a woman in a silk dress, in gold and silver, holding the symbols of a sword and a sponge, her hair pulled back in a dark bun. She was entirely defiant, her expression serious and yet somehow teasing, baiting. Was she asking for confrontation? Was she asking to sacrifice herself? Was she asking, after all this, for more?

The man downstairs was not the last to take issue with us. Another paced around, then told Miranda off for taking a photo of an etching. More huffed and stormed out. The men were triggered; there was a funny feeling in the air. We smiled to one another, rolled our eyes, looked the men in the eye when they complained to us, did not move. Surely Rego would enjoy this: how quickly her audience mimicked her own work, how we all submitted to her art, one way or another. How we became disciples of Rego.

We walked out of the gallery and towards the train station, through the cold. We talked about Sam's poetry and his book coming out. Miranda was quiet today, introspective. We compared Edinburgh and Glasgow like we always did. "Everyone keeps moving there, which is annoying," Sam said. "Maybe you two should," I suggested, though I knew they wouldn't.

At Haymarket, I rushed to catch the train to Glasgow. It was warm inside, the lights almost amber, too strong. I took off my hat and gloves and scarf, two of my layers. The girl across from me was sullen, eating a sausage roll and wearing headphones. I sat back, wanted to sleep, closed my eyes. As I did, I saw that painting, *Angel* — her sword and her sponge. Her face. Her strength. Could she be my guardian angel? I would like that.

I remembered the *Abortion Triptych*, and elsewhere, a pregnant woman, and elsewhere, an annoyed woman. *What Men Have Done To Us*, they seemed to say, in their figures alone, bearing witness to silent transgressions. *What We Have Done*

To Ourselves. I remembered being younger, weaker, stronger. Always reacting to something a man had done, minutes of recklessness and complacent violence, passive cruelty.

Later on, back in my flat, my son asleep, I went back to Rego's work, flicking through the exhibition catalogue. Over and over again, these strong, stubborn faces, and the unconditional loyalty and love that they expressed. The purest, most visceral religion she offered here. I could only bow to that. I wanted her religion. To be mastered by it, freed by it. I only wanted that.

I took out my pencils and paper and kept drawing until I was peaceful again, like I was praying. I prayed to Paula Rego's Angel: please watch over me, please see me, as I see you. She cut through my fear with her sword, cleansed me of that endemic shame and despair. I slept, relaxed.

—

Back in Glasgow, I continued with the drawing. I drew dark shadows, I drew friends, the friends I had loved so much. The friends who were leaving or would leave or were already gone.'I drew strangers in bars, men who played on my mind, those I was close to, or had been. I drew my own shadows, entangled with theirs. I drew my son.

I kept drawing until I was peaceful again, like I was praying to Saints. I prayed to Paula Rego's Angel again. I prayed to Robert Mapplethorpe, for persistence. I prayed to Egon Schiele, for fearlessness. I prayed to Francesca Woodman, for grace. I drew myself back into life, having been erased.

Gradually, the crisis that had subsumed me subsided. With drawing — marking the page with a simple physical action, making something new — I dug away at a new world, realised something fresh. As the paintings and drawings built up, I could see myself, and the world, anew. Grief, trauma and motherhood had overwhelmed me, and brought out the moods that were perhaps always my predisposition. But in these moods there was strength, too; with this cyclical process that seemed to be innate to my experience of life, I could also trust that things would always change. Drawing and printmaking actualised that innate cycle; it gave me a way to be at peace with the ups and downs, the darkness of remembering, the surrealism of claiming your own body when others, whether creatively or destructively, have claimed it as their own.

After you have grown a new life inside you, and dedicated your body and mind to the task of nourishing this new being, how can you think of your own body as truly "yours" anymore? When you have been violated or abused, how can you reclaim your sense of ownership of your own body? And when you have watched someone you love die from a long, brutal illness — physically disappearing over time — how can you reconcile your own sense of being? How can you overcome the anxiety that comes with this sort of confrontation with mortality? This hovering threat that life can disappear — that you can disappear — so quickly?

Drawing and knowing other artists and images enabled me to reconcile with these great anxieties and the experiences that caused them, ultimately finding a way to live with this strange, surreal sense of what it is to be human. Being "me" does not mean being isolated and secure and safe; it means being resilient enough to exist through this ever-changing sense of embodiment and disembodiment, where other people and events do take and dominate and disappear and turn away. It is to understand that loss — of other people and even ourselves — is part of living. Grief is within us, just as the ability to nourish others is too. We are more fluid than we admit sometimes, and so, too, more connected to everyone else.

Through conversation and practice, I found a way to reconcile myself to this life, and to the pain of loving and losing others. By drawing, I found a way to reappear despite everything, to be visible to myself again. I found a way to articulate and visualise the pain of losing others, and how I existed with and through them, as they did through me. Art became not a solace as such, but a way to exist and emerge, a part of living, a form of strength. It was Paula Rego's Angel, a spiritual calling, a ritual as everyday and necessary as cooking and sleeping and waking. A way of life.

—

Towards the end of summer, I started another painting, taking inspiration from the Eduardo Paolozzi print I had framed in the living room, with the words: *"Intimate Confessions — I was a rich man's plaything"*. I wanted to create my own version, reclaim the sentiment, in a way. I painted the same pin-up figure, but her face was blurred and haunted, pastel shades fading into one another, so her expression was ghost-like and ambiguous, intangible. I painted the red cherries and a blur of dirty pale pink over a bright turquoise. Lolita had taken up the frame as her own; the words and advertising were gone. She was confused and intangible, blurred and dazed, alone, but she held herself unapologetically. *Look at me.* I scrawled, in a body, a face, a bed. *Look at me.*

I thought again about being disconnected and emotionally unavailable, in the past — the very characteristics that had tormented me in other people. But then I thought of my son and my friends, one in particular. And we had connected, hadn't we? Maybe romantic situations were still an Achilles heel, but friendship was a start. Did I sometimes feel like a vampire? Yes. But had my friends and son succeeded in dragging me into the sun? Yes. And it was not so bad. I had not burnt yet, anyway. I could live in the light places too. I thought of them and then bell hooks again, *all about love*, and it clicked. I had all the love. I had fought hard for the love and despite everything, I had all the love. It had never truly gone. I was love and they were love and we had everything we needed.

—

After school started, his father came back to Glasgow more regularly, once a month usually, and spent a couple of days there. It meant I could go out a little more, work a little more. It meant he was releasing me from the past, in a small but nevertheless important way, gradually enabling me to emerge from the isolated state that meant I could barely leave the house until now. It meant he could see his son more, crucially. It meant that family was less splintered, less broken, for our son. It meant, I hoped, that we were both moving on.

I hadn't wanted to think that all the pain and grief I had been experiencing, this summer and the one before, had anything to do with the divorce. I didn't want to sit with that pain, I wanted to sign it away in a single legal document and be done with it. I dwelled on every other trauma I had been through, rather than accept that the end of my marriage, the breaking up of this family, had broken my heart. Why had I cared so much about my grandmother, who I had never met? Because she was a young mother whose marriage was also over, who had fallen for someone else and found herself alone and terrified and ostracised. She had thought there to be no way out. She drank and self-medicated herself to death. Why had I stayed in Scotland for so long, if not to stay with the memories? Of all that was over now? Why did I punish myself so badly? I could not contain the grief anymore. I let it contain me instead.

But then summer came. I could not resist summer any more than I had once tried to resist winter. These cycles would happen despite my own will. I could not flinch from the sunshine forever. The grief had started seeping out, the tension releasing itself, the world reappearing to me once again. I drew more. A bed. A couple. Bars. Men in bars, and me. Girls. More of the same, more of the same lines and floors and eyes. Him. His face, starting to emerge into my life. His eyes.

I fell in love like I fell into shapes in the room, into the lines of faces I knew too well, into an openness and optimism I had forgotten could be so convincing, so true, so close. Drawing was love, the first love, and it drew me here, a shark on the end of the line, biting free.

I realised, over the next couple of years — in which I repeated myself and my patterns over and over again, as I fell deeper in love again, and summer turned to winter again, and then back and forth — that on a deeper level, my fear concealed what felt like an endless longing, and it often distracted me from it too. I had been missing a huge chunk of myself that I had been suppressing out of fear; it meant that I always felt at a loss. I had always been lost, at sea.

I longed for many things I had repressed in myself, but perhaps the most, I missed being feminine. That may seem strange, as superficially I probably always seemed feminine enough, but emotionally I felt there was always a pressure to be strong, to become hardened and imperceptible, to always have to take all the responsibility, to always have to be the reliable one. I missed being able to let go, being able to be weakened, being able to be soft, to lose control, to have no pressure to be in control.

Over time, I realised that I needed to feel safe to feel that way, to fully allow that part of myself to exist. It had been shamed and punished out of me for so many years, for most of my life really. I had felt this need to hide away, not simply to protect myself, but because other people, those who should have been closest to me, were so easily intimidated. I had grown up in an atmosphere in which to be fully myself was not wanted, not allowed, and would be shamed and punished should I dare to. And so, eventually, I realised that beneath my sense of fearfulness was actually a longing to reconnect with that side of myself — to reach and embody a softer side, to enjoy the feminine power I had been turned away from, not because I was afraid of it, because it had made other people afraid, and I had feared their violent reactions.

It took until very recently to fully understand this longing, which also meant a need to find and develop relationships that would enable me to nurture that part of myself, and to be that way, instead of having to repress it or apologise for it, or take on merely the role of a caretaker so as not to threaten the fragile egos of others. I had to accept their rejection of me, and with their rejection eventually came, strangely, a true sense of peace.

Fearfulness, the embodied projections of other people's fragile egos, this tailoring myself to the lives and whims of others, had erased the essence of myself and so much else. This repression caused me so much longing and so much pain. I was tired of being on guard, or having to explain myself, or having to be scared. I was tired, still, of being heartbroken, but I knew better how others relied on this fracture of myself to feel better about themselves. There were so many vampires. I had turned faint and ghost-like myself.

I carved out a space for myself in my own life eventually, despite them and the masochistic echo in myself. In the simplest way, it meant letting go of those whom I could not relax around, or not be free around. It meant accepting the madness and sabotage of others and the disintegration of love and the loss of dreamt up things, the loss of seemingly once perfect things, the transience of that which had once seemed endless and perfect, and also accepting the faith I would, nevertheless, be fine. That I was also, by nature, transient. I could be peaceful even in times of turmoil, even after losing what I had cherished so deeply.

A Full Moon in Leo

A few days after signing the contract for this book with my publisher, I was hit by a motorbike while crossing the road. At the time, though in shock and quite traumatised, I joked that perhaps the book was cursed. Or perhaps God was sending me new material. It was certainly a double-edged sword. I didn't die, after all, and was not all that badly injured — just concussion, cuts and bruises all over my face and a very badly bruised and sprained knee. My son, who was holding my hand at the time, was miraculously unharmed. And so, although I had been unlucky in the sense I had been hit, we had been extremely lucky that it had been me and not him, and I was still alive.

Nevertheless, the experience stayed with me as I finished writing this book, about three years after that particular phase of my life had ended, and it crystallised my thinking about fear. One of the first thoughts I had had, while hobbling away, was that in the moments before I was hit, I had been distracted by my own anxiety, about my boyfriend, and that had made me more vulnerable to being struck. I had been living in a severe state of stress in the months before, and though I had been careful to look out for traffic, perhaps, I thought, I had missed the oncoming vehicle because my thoughts were too quick and impatient. I was living in such a constant state of fear and stress that I could not adequately realise the much graver threat coming right at me.

This is the problem with anxiety, with the Fear, with this

state of mind. When everything is stressful and threatening, the most severe and immediate threats lose their impact. So I became more vulnerable, not less, for all my worrying. I nearly died. My son — the most important person in my life, the deepest love and my greatest responsibility — could also have died. The Fear — and not anything it told me I needed to worry about — was in itself the threat.

Such fear, and the state of mind it affects, has a way of weakening you, of blinding you to the reality of threat levels and of distracting you in a perpetual, exhausting war. This distraction is key in political life just as much as personal life; I began to see how such distraction by diffuse fears like the threat of terrorism could so easily disorientate and confuse people so that they would not see the immediate, serious threats right in front of them.

As Lars Svendsen points out, "fear robs us of our freedom"[49] and in particular, "a crucial part of our political freedom is living our lives without too much fear".[50] If we are constantly being intimidated by threats, whether real or imagined or exaggerated, if there is this wider culture of fear, then any decisions we make will be more likely to be knee-jerk reactions based on fight or flight responses and misplaced anxiety. We will not see the motorbike coming around the corner; we will be more vulnerable than ever.

Fear can be both constructive and destructive; it can break you down, but it can also open up a new, better relationship with the world.[51] Some danger and risk is necessary for the

49   Lars Svendsen, *A Philosophy of Fear,* 127.

50   Ibid. 123.

51   Jean Delumeau, *Sin and Fear: The Emergence of a Western Guilt Culture,*
     13th–18th Centuries. Translated by Eric Nicholson. New York: St. Martin's
     Press, 1990.

enjoyment of life and personal and societal progress. It all depends on how that fear is processed and the wider context of how we experience emotions, and how they are controlled and communicated at a societal level.

Ultimately, the only way to free ourselves from endemic fearfulness and related manipulation of such primal (and often justified) instincts is to develop, in ourselves and one another, true courage, optimism and camaraderie in the face of persistent threat and uncertainty. There is a difference, crucially, between acknowledging and feeling fear, and succumbing to it, defeated. There is also a difference between a state of perennial, often misplaced fear, and simply reacting to serious, immediate threats as and when they appear — and then pitying one's bullies, those who use manipulation, lies and intimidation to control you, for they have nothing else.

So can we learn to live with our fears and wounds and yet live victoriously and nobly? Can we be truly courageous in our compassion and care for one another, choosing to love and engage in a world that presents so many reasons to turn from it and one another? Can we still love the world and all it offers even when we are surrounded by corrupt and opportunistic manipulators? Crucially, what boundaries — personal, ethical and political — must we put up in order to navigate and rise above politics and dominance of fear? How can we love other people when there is so much to be afraid of, and so much to lose?

Trust is crucial in personal and political relationships, to balance out what drains our efforts and ideals. Trust can mitigate our fears and alter our worldview so that, although threats remain and the world is a precarious place, we can trust one another to the point where the stability we have built balances out excessive insecurity. The old values of community, solidarity and camaraderie can bolster us against a nihilistic worldview and help us see that we can rely on one another even in terrible and traumatic situations. Suffering is part of life for us all, and certainly it can be shouldered by more of us, more equally, in many situations.

Fear signifies that we have something to live for. We can balance inevitable fear of loss, death, pain and loneliness with the fortitude of hope, bravery, intimacy and love. We can own the anger and eroticism that we are told to quieten for the benefit of those who would like to diminish us. The Fear I have written of is a consequence of a nihilistic, splintered and traumatised world, and only by acknowledging and healing the deeper wounds of our society and ourselves is it possible to live better and more courageously. Though it takes courage to endure fear, manipulation and the pain that accompanies it, it takes more courage to fight, transcend and then finally let it go.

There are all sorts of ways of living with fear that do not entail violence and division. It all comes down to accepting reality, I think, and asserting stability and peace in the face of chaos and angst, and the ideals and visions — the utopian imagination that would otherwise be crushed — in the face of restriction and repression. In politics, the gaslighting and lying, the disorientation committed intentionally to weaken us, can be minimised by a stubborn insistence on facts, reality and the validity of our own experiences and lives. Violence, like psychological abuse, works to deny other people's reality — and our ability to imagine any other reality — so that the perpetrator will feel comparatively more powerful. While from a victim's perspective that assault or abuse may be unavoidable, there is nevertheless scope to recover and defend oneself by simply acknowledge and defending one's own validity and life, the reality of oneself, without recourse to retaliation and more violence. It is possible to reclaim idealism and vision, to build something closer to the utopia we are told cannot exist, to expand on what we are conditioned to think so that we may move toward true happiness and meaning and freedom.

It is easy to think of religion as one more form of escapism, and to think of art in this way too, but as I understand it, though there may be tendencies for this to be true, religion and art both offer systems of camaraderie and validation that are valuable; they can help us accept the validity of human nature, of human weakness and the need to be loved and cared for. Even if you are dying, if you know you are truly loved and accepted for who you are, you will not be scared.

Religion and art offer this sort of idealistic, spiritual and yet everyday love, and of course we can simply offer it to one another too. In writing this book, in which I have repeatedly faced my various fears, which I dwelled on for so many years already, it is what I keep returning to. Fear is inevitable and persistent and a mark of being human, because the world, and our existence within it, is and always will be precarious. To deny that is futile. But to ground oneself in the real love that also exists, in whichever way one finds it, is also in our reality, and it is as persistent and available as fear, shame and detachment. The only real way to move beyond fight-or-flight responses, the compulsions, harms and violence they inspire, and the toxic political systems that rely on such fearfulness, is to remain attached to that quiet, endless defiance that is more powerful than the worst crimes committed in the depths of panic and weakness.

So perhaps, then, I divert from Nietzsche's influence in the end. I realise the value now in coming to terms with weakness, in forgiving those who are also weak, even as they abuse their power or take whatever power they can, and even as they hurt and destroy. The Fear I have written about is part of being human, as alienating and disassociating as it may feel. It is part of human nature to wrestle with it and to take it out on one another, and also to question whether we are ever really going through it together.

I think that is the greatest fear — that we are truly alone in this world, that the relationships and ideas we have are merely illusions, that we cannot trust in any form of true emotional security, and so we are compelled to grasp for alternatives desperately. But we are not really alone, although the fear of that loneliness, ironically, can isolate us further. But this fear is what unites us as well as what divides us; we all experience it. We are all going to die, and lose people, and suffer pain and disillusionment, regardless of the barriers we put up. Power, and the attempts to be more powerful than others, are a way of deflecting from this reality. But no wealth or physical violence will change this reality.

At the beginning of this book, I wrote about heartbreak and my tendency to replace one heartbreak with another, almost compulsively, to conceal from myself the deeper heartbreaks that I had experienced. What could be more heart-breaking than a parent dying, or a loved one leaving, or a deep betrayal of trust from someone you believed in and loved? What could be more destabilising and traumatic than a random act of violence from a total stranger? What could be more shattering? The Fear, in all its manifestations and variations, is a scrambled attempt to negate the pain of that reality in order to survive — however chaotic the consequences may be — when reality feels overwhelming and insurmountable.

I think the only way forward, and the antidote to the emotional pain at the heart of this state, which is also, at root, an existential crisis — that reality is not as we had hoped, that reality is just a set of fragile illusions — is simply to keep asserting that love and compassion are nevertheless real too. Lies, loss and cruelty are all part of life, and the threat of those things is part of life too, but we should not let the endurance of that pain eclipse everything else that remains and matters, however difficult it may be to hang on to any such optimism and conviction in times of real terror. When I stood up after the motorbike hit me and saw that my son was fine, I knew all at once that at the root of my fear was unconditional love.

Rather than allow myself to be weakened by my own vulnerability, I try now to remind myself that such love is also the greatest strength and the root of resilience, everyone's resilience; it is the reason to keep living, and why fear exists at all. I try to allow myself to find such pleasure and meaning in that love, not just the fear that I could lose it. I am grateful for every day we have together.

———

In the months after the motorbike accident, and a traumatic breakup that followed three days later, as I lay in bed concussed and injured; whilst then, after that, I finished this book, I leant on my friends. Their love and kindness revived me from the depths of despair and disillusionment, the worst void of heartbreak. One talked to me at midnight when I was crying about it, even though he was on a night out; another gave me make-up to cover the bruises; others danced with me at Halloween, one wearing a crow as a hat. They involved me, drew me in to the rest of my life, which I might otherwise have forgotten.

One of them, Lana, invited me to a Full Moon crystal workshop with her friend Rose, who was also an artist, the last weekend of December, just before Christmas, which I was spending alone with my son for the third time in our life together, and which I was nervous about, still wanting it to be a fun day, rather than lonely and sad.

We had to do the crystal workshop on Zoom because of all the Covid restrictions, so I found myself at my laptop, having arranged some candles and the few crystals I possessed around it, in a strange digital shrine. I logged on and saw these little rectangles of people, in mostly dimly lit rooms, with their crystals and candles around them.

My own crystals were mostly random — a quartz angel that my mother-in-law had given me when I was first pregnant. A purple heart that my own mother had given me, though I wasn't especially into crystals at the time. And then there was the pendant I had picked up that morning, in a strange, charged transaction down by the canal. I had walked past a stall in Camden and got talking to a girl, and as I picked up several different crystals, she said they were all versions of the same type of crystal, so I must be drawn to it for a reason. It was Labradorite, known as a magical representation of the Aurora Borealis, or the Northern Lights. I started telling her about growing up in Scotland, in the woods, and how I missed it. "You should go back to the rituals of your childhood," she said. "What might they be?"

"We made a lot of bonfires," I said. "Sometimes, I'd write things down I wanted to be rid of, and burn them in the fire. And it would help… I suppose London isn't the best place for a bonfire, but maybe… Maybe I could find some candles." She smiled, and a few hours later, I was sitting in this virtual group, with candles and the Labradorite.

In the ritual, we were guided through a sort of meditation, eyes closed, music playing. We had been told there would be a snow queen, and she would have a message for us, after we climbed a frozen mountain. I saw various people from my past and my family… and then, the ice queen, perhaps a mixture of them all, perhaps something else, perhaps a part of myself.

"I'm sorry I threw you away," the ice queen said. "But you'll be happier in the water." And then I was in the water, in a warm place, and I was a mermaid, and a man was in a boat smiling at me, and he was happy for me too. And somehow, I was not sure how — we manifested it, this scenario of mermaids and peacefulness — and this led to my being in almost this exact situation, just a couple of moon cycles later.

—

I flew into Los Angeles on another full moon — in Leo, this time — and met Lana and Rose there. We all managed to get commissions or VIP passes for Frieze Week at the last minute; I was interviewing a painter and writing up a feature about the week in general.

The first exhibition I went to with Lana, straight from the airport, was serendipitously (given the crystal workshop vision) about mermaids. We wandered around videos and installations about these red-haired mermaids, against bright blue waves, jetlagged but happy.

Our Airbnb was a converted church with stained glass windows to the east of Beverly Hills, and we were sharing a pink bed overlooking a beautiful garden. In the mornings, we drank coffee at a large table under a green parasol, wearing sunglasses because it was already bright. Lana had a lot more energy than I did for going around all the exhibitions, but we went to a fair few together as well.

When I first arrived, one of the hosts told me that his wife, who was away caring for their newborn grandchild, was also an ordained minister and scholar, and she had left out her book to read, after Lana told them I had studied ritual and violence as well. Her book was on evil and redemption in the work of Lars Von Trier.[52] One night, when Lana had fallen

---

52 Rebecca Ver Straten-McSparran, *Lars von Trier's Cinema: Excess, Evil, and the Prophetic Voice*, Routledge (2021).

asleep, I stayed up and read as much of it as I could, taking pictures of my favourite passages and quotes.

One idea in particular stayed with me — the idea of "evil-scepticism", and especially the dismissal or deflection from cases of real evil, as a way of shrugging off the moral and spiritual dimension of so many of our problems. It was important to understand the existence of evil, but in particular to understand it as a form of weakness as well. To confront the real existence of human weakness as a cause of so much evil and all its horrific consequences, and also to rise above it. To believe in redemption and cleansing, as well as pain and fear. Not to analyse it away, or see it in a detached sense, but to really confront, wholly and spiritually, the existence of evil and how our lives pivot around a fear of that, and also, perhaps most crucially, a fear of fighting it and of believing in something greater.

I realised, as I read her book, that I had been afraid of something brighter too. I had been afraid that the love had not been real, that God was gone, that life was merely a cliff edge. But here, I saw that was not the case. In seeing so much weakness, I could no longer deny strength where I felt and saw it too.

Rebecca quoted Andrei Tarkovsky in her book: "The artist, too, is driven by a kind of instinct, and his work furthers man's search for what is eternal, transcendent, divine — often in spite of the sinfulness of the poet himself."[53]

—

---

53   Andrei Tarkovsky, *Sculpting in Time,* University of Texas Press, 1989.

On the last day in LA, I went to a talk with Rose, introducing a painting and jewellery collaboration called *Armour of Light, Heart of Clay* by Brazilian artist Samuel de Saboia and jewellery design studio Alighieri. He had created a huge mural that responded to Dante's *Inferno,* which was paired with talismanic, ritualistic pendants on display around the room. He talked about creating a vision of transformative feminine energy that would heal and embolden, in his figurative paintings, in their red and their rose pink. Here, the soul's journey into the rings of the bad place could be a hopeful and healing one, he seemed to say. This hellscape was also the city of angels.

At the end, we were given a little goody bag, and each person had a different pendant. Rose had a lion, for courage, for Leo. I opened up my little box and found I had been given a golden, full moon. "The full moon ritual!" I said to Rose, and she smiled. Here it was. Full circle. The strangest, most complete, otherworldly love. I strung it around my neck; we went on our way, an inferno in shades of pink and red behind us. We left the beautiful hell in the burning sun, clutching talismans, iced coffees.

—

After I got back from LA, I realised that something had shifted profoundly. For the first time in my life, I didn't feel a crushing anxiety, a sense of being invisible and non-existent. I was content, not scared. I took far more joy in looking after my plants and cooking and swimming, in basic things, and our life relaxed.

Perhaps writing this book had helped, in some way, and the drawing and the painting, and the rituals, and close friends. I cried in front of Lana for the first time, another night out, and she wiped my tears away, and I understood I didn't have to do everything by myself anymore.

A few weeks later I went to Glasgow with my son for another exhibition, and for three days between hanging and the opening we visited the Isle of Bute. We arrived into a mist, but the sky brightened the next day. We walked on the beach and picked up little rocks of rose quartz and took photos of the beautiful sea all around us, so calm and glistening. He found a map and showed me another tiny island to the south-west of Bute. "It's called 'Wee Island.'. That's its name! Isn't that cute?" he said. "It is cute," I replied. "Very cute." "That's like you and me," he said. "Bute and Wee Island. Bute-iful! And Wee Island." We laughed and he threw more rocks into the sea, skimming the gentle water.

After a few days we went back to the mainland on the ferry, back to Glasgow and then, eventually, back to London. I kept the rose quartz from the beach in my pocket and he held my other hand. We were not scared, but happy. I felt the smooth rose quartz in one hand and his warm little hand in the other and I was grounded and we were content, and in these moments I feared nothing at all. We were out of the Underworld now, we were in a deeper light. The moon glowed pink and pure, weathered but light and soft from its years of erosion, coveted and found and loved.

Caspian

Bibliography

André, Jacques, "Immanent Masochism", in the *European Journal of Psychoanalysis, trans. Claudia Vaughn.*

Apel, Dora and Smith, Shawn Michelle, *Lynching Photographs,* University of California Press, 2007.

Bauman, Zygmunt, *Liquid Fear,* University of Cambridge Press, 2006. 3, quoted in Butler, Judith, *Frames of War,* 2009.

Bloom, Paul, *The Sweet Spot: The Pleasures of Suffering and the Search for Meaning,* Ecco Books, 2021.

Camus, Albert, *The Myth of Sisyphus*, Penguin 2005

Cantalupo, Barbara, *Poe and the Visual Arts,* Penn State University Press, 2014.

Connell, R. W., *Masculinities,* Berkeley, California: University of California Press, 1995.

Cowart, Leigh, *Hurts So Good: The Science and Culture of Pain on Purpose,* PublicAffairs, 2021.

Delumeau, Jean, *Sin and Fear: The Emergence of a Western Guilt Culture, 13th–18th Centuries.* Translated by Eric Nicholson. New York: St. Martin's Press, 1990.

Dimitriadis, Yorgos, "The Psychoanalytic Concept of Jouissance and the Kindling Hypothesis" in *Frontiers in Psychology*, 21 September 2017.

Dimitriadis, Yorgos, "The Psychoanalytic Concept of Jouissance and the Kindling Hypothesis" in *Frontiers in Psychology*, 21 September 2017.

Douglas, Mary, *Purity and Danger,* Routledge, 1966.

Dworkin, Andrea. *Pornography: Men Possessing Women*, The Women's Press Ltd., 1981.

Elshtain, J. B., "Just War as Politics: What the Gulf War Told Us About Contemporary American Life", in D. E. Decosse (ed.), *But Was It Just? Reflections on the Morality of the Persian Gulf War*, New York: Doubleday, 1992.

Evans, Debbie, "Sartre and Beauvoir on Hegel's Master-Slave dialectic and the question of the "look" (2009)

Foster, Dawn, *Lean Out*, Repeater Books, 2016.

Frayling, Christopher, "Fuseli's The Nightmare: Somewhere between the Sublime and the Ridiculous," in *Gothic Nightmares: Fuseli, Blake, and the Romantic Imagination*, London: Tate Publishing, 2006.

Freeman, Lauren and Elpidorou, Andreas, 'Fear, Anxiety and Boredom,' in *The Routledge Handbook of Phenomenology of Emotions*, ed. T. Szanto & H. Landweer. New York: Routledge, 2020

Goldin, Nan, *The Ballad of Sexual Dependency*, 1986. Aperture; Revised ed. edition, 2012.

hooks, bell, *All About Love: New Visions (Love Song to the Nation)*, William Morrow, 2016.

Hegel, G. W. F., *The Phenomenology of Spirit*. Oxford University Press, U.S.A.; Revised ed. edition, 30 Nov. 1976.

Hutchisson, James, *Poe*, Jackson: University Press of Mississippi, 2005.

Jenkins, Brian Michael, *The New Age of Terrorism*, RAND, 2006.

Juergensmeyer, Mark, *Terror in the Mind of God: The Global Rise of Religious Violence*. 2000.

Kant, Immanuel, *Kritikk av dommekraften*, trans. Espen Hammer, Oslo, 1995, quoted in Lars Svenden, *A Philosophy of Fear*, London: Reaktion Books, 2009.

Leader, Darian, *Jouissance: Sexuality, Suffering and Satisfaction*, Polity, 2021

Lloyd, Genevieve, "Masters, Slaves and Others", *Radical Philosophy* 034, Summer 1983.

Lorde, Audre, *The Master's Tools Will Never Dismantle The Master's House*, Penguin Classics, 2018.

MacKinnon, Catherine A., *Are Women Human? And Other International Dialogues.* Harvard University Press, 2007.

Maté, Gabor, *When the Body Says No: The Cost of Hidden Stress,* Vermillion, 2019.

Moeller, Susan, *Shooting War: Photography and the American Experience of Combat,* Basic Books Inc., New York, 1989.

Moreland, Clark T. and Rodriguez, Karime, *The Edgar Allan Poe Review*, Vol. 16, No. 2, Autumn 2015.

Nietzsche, Friedrich, *Beyond Good and Evil.* Penguin Classics; Reissue edition, 2003.

Nietzsche, Friedrich, *Nachgelassene Fragmente 1884-1885,* in *Kritische Studienausgabe,* vol. xi, Munich, Berlin and New York, 1988.

Niva, S., "Tough and Tender: New World Order Masculinity and the Gulf War", in M. Zalewski and J. Parpart (eds), *The "Man" Question in International Relations,* Boulder, CO: Westview Press, 1998.

Ogilvy, James, "Mastery and Sexuality: Hegel's Dialectic in Sartre and Post-Freudian Psychology", *Human Studies* 3, 201-219, 1980.

Poe, Edgar Allen, "The Black Cat" in *The Portable Edgar Allen Poe,* Penguin Classics, 2006.

Richardson, Louise, *What Terrorists Want: Understanding the Terrorist Threat,* John Murray, 2006.

Rilke, Rainer Maria, *Duineser Elegien,* Munich, 1997, quoted in Lars Svenden, *A Philosophy of Fear,* London: Reaktion Books, 2009.

Scheff, Thomas A., *Catharsis in Healing, Ritual and Drama,* University of California Press, 1979.

Siep, Ludwig, "Hegel on the Master Slave Relation," *Fifteen Eight Four: Academic Perspectives from Cambridge University Press,* 2014.

Sjoberg, Laura & Gentry, Caron, *Mothers, Monsters, Whores: Women's Violence in Global Politics.* London and New York: Zed Books, 2007.

Sontag, Susan, *Regarding the Pain of Others*, Penguin, 2004.

Smith, Patti, *Just Kids*, Ecco Press, 2010.

Tarkovsky, Andrei, *Sculpting in Time*, University of Texas Press, 1989.

Ver Straten-McSparran, Rebecca, *Lars von Trier's Cinema: Excess, Evil, and the Prophetic Voice*, Routledge, 2021.

Svendsen, Lars, *A Philosophy of Fear*, Reaktion Books, 2008.

Van Der Kolk, Besser, *The Body Keeps the Score: Brain, Mind and Body in the Healing of Trauma*, Penguin Books, 2015.

Acknowledgements

Thank you so much to the Repeater team — Tariq Goddard, Josh Turner, Katie King and Ben Clarke, as well as the wider Watkins team, especially Etan Ilfeld, Karen Smith, Vicky Hartley, Adam Gordon, Laura Whittaker-Jones, Monica Mistry, Rahel Araya and Vikki Scott, for all your hard work and support.

I would also like to thank the Society of Authors, who kindly awarded me a grant to finish my book, as well as to Mind Camden for allowing me to access emotional support during the last year of this writing process. In particular, thank you to Susannah Tomkinson, who was such a great source of support and encouragement during this time.

I am grateful to to my friends and family, especially Francine Toon, Jenni Fagan, Joe Passmore, Charlie Gilmour, Ant Lehane, Lana Locke, Rosemary Cronin, Kate Hodal, Michaela Friedman, Nina Ellis, Geraldine Anderson, Christina Wolf, Tally de Orellana, Dylan Trigg, Audrey Petit and Karin Patek — thank you for all your inspiration, kindness, conversation and at times inspiration, however difficult.

Thank you to Orla Lynch and Caron Gentry, both former supervisors at St Andrews, for your guidance and encouragement throughout my PhD. Also thank you to Pablo de Orellana, Mariah Whelan, and Tom de Freston — our work together at Kings, and your friendship, was invaluable in steering my own ideas and creative work over the past few years. Thank you to Sophie Parkin, for giving me space to exhibit my work at Vout-O-Reenee's. And to Karen Mailley in Glasgow and Taisir Gibreel in Edinburgh, The Freud Museum in London and The Tartu Literary House in Estonia for supporting my work during this period. I am also so grateful to Andrew Gallix, Sam Mills, and Thom Cuell, as well as Miguel Benavides and Martin Kennedy at *Studio International*, Lucy Binnersley at *The London Magazine*, Jacob Wolff at *The Florida Review*, and Marina Benjamin at *Psyche*, who gave important feedback to earlier essays printed in their publications, which then formed part of this book. I'm also immensely grateful to Rob Doyle and Lily Dunn for reading early copies of the book and giving their kind support and camaraderie.

Thank you mostly to my son Caspian, who has always been by my side, and the sweetest companion I could ever hope for.

REPEATER BOOKS

is dedicated to the creation of a new reality. The landscape of twenty-first-century arts and letters is faded and inert, riven by fashionable cynicism, egotistical self-reference and a nostalgia for the recent past. Repeater intends to add its voice to those movements that wish to enter history and assert control over its currents, gathering together scattered and isolated voices with those who have already called for an escape from Capitalist Realism. Our desire is to publish in every sphere and genre, combining vigorous dissent and a pragmatic willingness to succeed where messianic abstraction and quiescent co-option have stalled: abstention is not an option: we are alive and we don't agree